RMS QUEEN ELIZABETH 2
THE LAST GREAT LINER

AMBERLEY

Queen Elizabeth 2

RMS QUEEN ELIZABETH 2

THE LAST GREAT LINER

JANETTE MCCUTCHEON

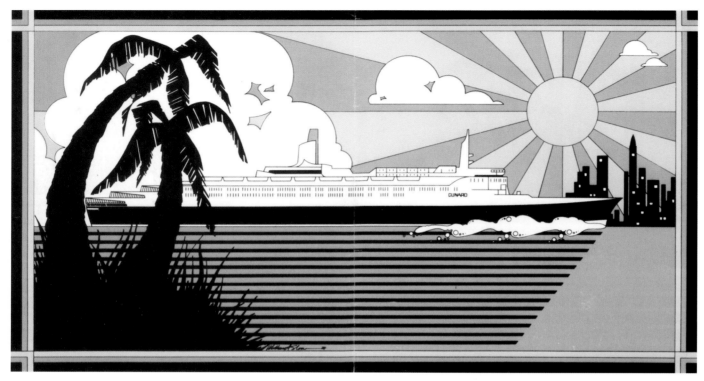

First published 2006, second revised edition, 2008

Amberley Publishing Plc
Cirencester Road, Chalford,
Stroud, Gloucestershire, GL6 8PE
www.amberley-books.com

British Library Cataloguing in Publication Data.
A catalogue record for this book is available from the British Library.

ISBN: 978 1 84868 055 5

Printed in Great Britain

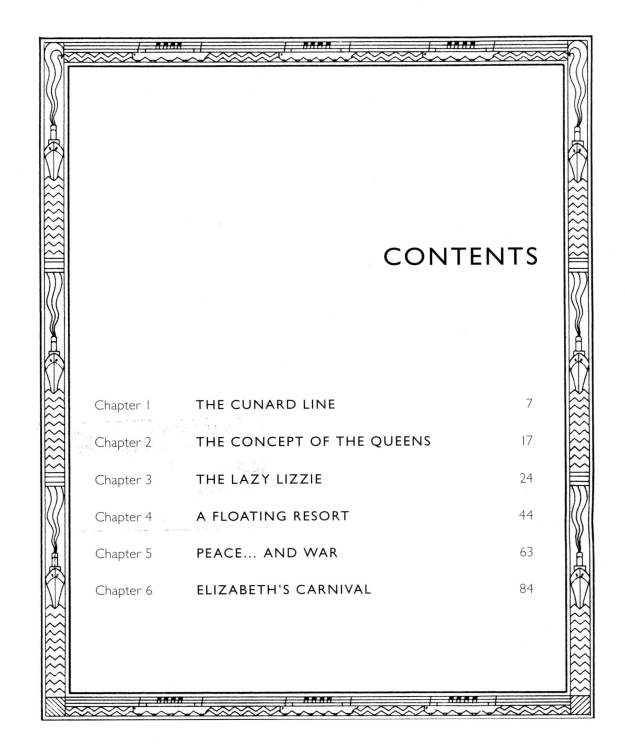

CONTENTS

Chapter I

THE CUNARD LINE

On a cold autumn day in 1967 a new era in transatlantic travel began. It was the age of the Jet, but Cunard, against all expectations and even common sense, was building a new transatlantic liner. Her name was a closely guarded secret until the reigning monarch launched her on 20 September 1967. Hull 736, the new Cunarder, gracefully slid down the slipway at Upper Clyde Shipbuilders' Clydebank yard and into the River Clyde. It was just two days after her older sister RMS *Queen Mary* had left on her final transatlantic voyage after 1,001 transatlantic voyages and thirty-one years of service, including six years of being a troopship.

Even as the new *Queen Elizabeth 2*, as Hull 736 was named, was being wrestled by tugs and being towed into moorings to be fitted out, optimism, but also uncertainty, surrounded her future – optimism because she was a new British liner, named by the Her Majesty Queen Elizabeth, the current monarch and because she was of the best of British quality; but uncertainty too, because the new jet age was haemorrhaging transatlantic liner trade and travelling by sea was no longer *de rigueur*. The new *Queen Elizabeth 2* though had an impressive pedigree. Not only was she the third Cunard *Queen* liner, but she had almost 120 years of Cunard Line history and tradition behind her.

The Cunard Line was originally called the British & North American Royal Mail Steam Packet Company, but, as the name was so long, it eventually took the name of its founder. Samuel Cunard was a Nova Scotian entrepreneur and he set his sights on obtaining the British Government Mail Contract to North America. He had already won the mail contract to take mails from Britain to Newfoundland, Halifax, Boston and Bermuda using sailing ships, but he had an idea of an 'ocean railway', linking the old world with the new. This involved integrating railways and shipping to make sure that shipping schedules tied in with the railway timetables and that traffic flowed smoothly. The concept was that passengers would flow from the trains in Britain onto the new-fangled transatlantic steam ships and then, once the ship had arrived in North America, catch the connecting train or trains to their destination.

Integrated transport in the 1830s was an unfamiliar concept. At the time sailing ships were the dominant force on the seas, but sailing ships were not very reliable as they relied heavily on the weather to determine their speed and scheduling. Good weather was just as much a determining factor in their estimated arrival time as bad weather – no wind on a sunny day could delay a sailing ship just as much as a storm.

Opposite: Britannia leaves from Liverpool on her maiden voyage on 4 July 1840.

Right: On Britannia, fresh milk was supplied by a cow. The ship also carried hens and other animals.

Far right: A typical menu from Hibernia, an early Cunarder.

Below: The early Cunard vessels really were tiny in comparison to even Mauretania.

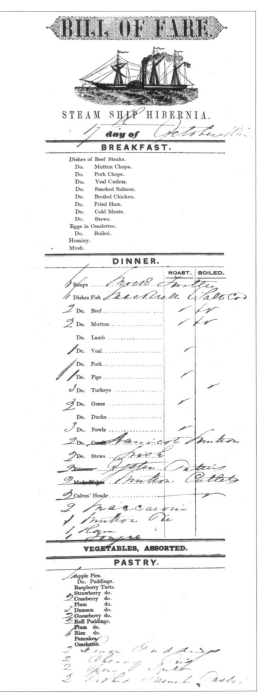

BILL OF FARE.

STEAM SHIP HIBERNIA.

day of October 1845

BREAKFAST.

Dishes of Beef Steaks.
Do.   Mutton Chops.
Do.   Pork Chops.
Do.   Veal Cutlets.
Do.   Smoked Salmon.
Do.   Broiled Chicken.
Do.   Fried Ham.
Do.   Cold Meats.
Do.   Stews.
Eggs in Omelettes.
Do.   Boiled.
Hominy.
Mush.

DINNER.

		ROAST.	BOILED.
Soups			
Dishes Fish			
2 Do.	Beef		
2 Do.	Mutton		
Do.	Lamb		
1 Do.	Veal		
Do.	Pork		
1 Do.	Pigs		
3 Do.	Turkeys		
2 Do.	Geese		
Do.	Ducks		
3 Do.	Fowls		
2 Do.	Curries		
2 Do.	Stews		
	Fricassee		
2 Made Dishes			
3 Calves' Heads			

VEGETABLES, ASSORTED.

PASTRY.

Apple Pies.
Do.   Puddings.
Raspberry Tarts.
Strawberry do.
Cranberry do.
Plum do.
Damson do.
Gooseberry do.
Roll Puddings.
Plum do.
Rice do.
Pancakes.
Omelettes.

The *"Scotia"* and the *"Mauretania."*

Despite never losing a passenger's life at sea, Cunard still managed to lose some fine vessels to shipwreck. RMS *Malta* lies wrecked off the Cornish coast.

Ever the entrepreneur and forward-thinker, Samuel Cunard had had the foresight to invest in a ship called the *Royal William*. *Royal William* was built by Black & Campbell, shipbuilders, in Nova Scotia and was one of a new generation of ships designed to be able to cross the Atlantic totally under steam power. Steam power on the Atlantic had been around since 1819 when *Savannah* crossed the Atlantic in 29 days. She was powered by a mixture of steam and sail, but her coal ran out off the coast of Ireland and she had to sail the rest of the way. The first crossing of the Atlantic totally by steam was by the paddle steamer *Sirius*. *Sirius* crossed the Atlantic in 18 days. She would have been the first Blue Riband winner (awarded for the fastest crossing of the North Atlantic by steam ship) but the title did not exist for another sixty years!

When Samuel Cunard was looking for new steamships of his own for the recently-won mail contract, he crossed the Atlantic to Scotland. The shipyards of the River Clyde, near Glasgow, were at the forefront of shipbuilding technology. Reliable steamships had been built on the Clyde since 1812 when Henry Bell's paddle steamer *Comet* first

appeared, and the Clyde was already well known for its sailing ships. The shipyards of the Clyde built all types of steamships from passenger ships to paddle steamers, from naval ships and cargo ships to royal yachts. During the mid-nineteenth century, the Clyde was the best place to go for a steamship, and this was where Samuel Cunard headed.

Once the mail contract was awarded in May 1839, Cunard approached Robert Napier, the prestigious engineer and shipbuilder, to design and build the first Cunard ships. Although Cunard was only required to build three ships, Napier persuaded him to build four and to make them larger than the Admiralty specifications. Cunard was the largest investor in the new company with a share of £55,000. While he was in Scotland, several Scottish businessmen invested in the new steamship company to make up the capital shortfall. As well as the initial investors, the Admiralty gave a subsidy of £55,000 per year from the Admiralty for the mail contract. With a total capital of £270,000, the new British & North American Royal Mail Steam Packet Company was born. As a thank you to his investors, Cunard incorporated the Scottish Lion Rampant onto the company's logo – and it still remains there today.

The first ship off the stocks was *Britannia*. *Britannia* was of 1,154 tons, and was 207ft long and 34ft wide. She had a speed of 9 knots. Her maiden voyage was on Saturday, 4 July 1840 from Liverpool. Samuel Cunard and his daughter Ann were on board along with 65 passengers. The voyage took 11 days and 4 hours. Cunard insisted on safety first and then excellent service and soon the Cunard ships had a reputation for being the best on the high seas.

Cunard's next three ships – *Caledonia, Arcadia* and *Columbia* – were designed to be mail packets too. But as the steam packets were safer than sailing ships, more and more people began to request passage on them. This was good for Cunard, as the Line had another revenue earner; but other companies were set up to cash in on Cunard's success. Problems occurred for other companies as they ran their ships at full speed through storms and ice (and often lost them, such as the Collins Line with their *Arctic*). Many of these shipping lines did not have Government mail contracts and relied on passenger and cargo revenue for their profits.

As the years progressed, Cunard's fleet expanded and each ship was more beautiful than the previous one. Business opportunities opened up across the Atlantic and people wanted to cross quickly. With the old adage of 'time is money', they demanded faster sailing times and often chose to travel by the fastest ships. So ships accommodated this by becoming bigger, faster and with more luxurious fittings. The White Star Line added baths, electric lights and lifts to their ships. Along with this luxury for first-class passengers, shipping lines started adding space to their ships for emigrants. These emigrants were the real revenue earners, as lots of people could be accommodated in a small space. They did not pay much for their passage in comparison to first class, but a vast number of emigrants could be packed into a very small space and needed none of the complicated food and luxurious accommodation that their first-class counterparts enjoyed, making them far more profitable.

By the 1890s, the Cunard Line found itself competing with not only British shipping lines such as White Star, but also with foreign lines such as the Hamburg-Amerika, Holland-America and Red Star lines. Many of these newer lines had introduced speedier and more luxurious ships. As a result, Cunard had to keep building bigger and better ships to compete with them.

By 1902, the shipping world had changed and a company called International Mercantile Marine (IMM), and headed by the American financier, John Pierpoint Morgan, started buying up passenger shipping lines in an attempt to monopolise trade on the North Atlantic. IMM bought companies such as the American Line, Dominion Line, Holland America, F. Leyland & Co., and the Red Star Line. But they were after the two most famous lines on the Atlantic run, White Star and Cunard. Morgan eventually took over White Star, which worried Cunard as it was possible thast IMM would try to buy them next. The Admiralty was equally worried because if International Mercantile Marine took over the Cunard Line, then there would be no large British line remaining loyal to the British Government. This would mean a loss of troop-carrying capacity in the event of war.

Cunard used this fear to its advantage and managed to get a huge loan from the British Government to pay for and subsidise the operation of two large superliners, bigger and better and faster than anything else on the Atlantic run. It was agreed that the British Government would provide subsidies and loans for Cunard to build these new ships. In return, Cunard was to remain steadfastly British. In addition, incorporated into the design of these new ships would be the ability for them to be turned into troop carriers or warships in the event of war. Originally designed as three funnelled vessels, the two new ships were to become the four-funnelled *Mauretania* and *Lusitania*. At almost 34,000 gross registered tons, the two vessels, one constructed on Tyneside and the other on the Clyde, were a full third larger again than any other ship in the world, and both were provided with massive steam turbines and four propellers to help power them to speeds in excess of 25kt, faster than any large ship in existence.

White Star announced as the *Lusitania* and *Mauretania* were entering service that they were going to construct two even larger vessels; *Olympic* and *Titanic*. In this peacetime race for supremacy, the German Hamburg Amerika Line replied with ultra-luxurious ships called *Imperator*, *Vaterland* and *Bismarck*.

The first of the two new Cunard giants was *Lusitania*. Built on the Clyde at John Brown's shipyard, she was the pride of the British fleet. Her sister, *Mauretania*, built at Swan Hunter & Wigham Richardson's soon followed. These ships soon captured the crème of the North Atlantic trade and became the darlings of the society set. For the rich and famous, travelling on the fastest and most luxurious ship was the equivalent to being seen at the right clubs or at the most prestigious society events.

When the First World War began in 1914, the Cunard ships were still carrying civilian passengers across the Atlantic. *Lusitania* was sunk by a German U-Boat in May 1915 with the loss of over 1,000 lives. *Mauretania* was turned into an armed merchant cruiser, then a troop transport and a hospital ship and survived the war relatively unscathed. A third four-funnelled Cunard giant, *Aquitania*, had just been completed a bare three months before war started and she too served in the war as a troopship and hospital ship.

Although steam power was a feature of Cunard vessels, they were all fitted with auxiliary sail until the 1880s. *Etruria* under sail in the early 1890s.

Above: A busy scene at Liverpool. *Campania* leaves for New York.

Right: Campania or *Lucania* at the Landing Stage, Liverpool.

Below: Caronia at Madeira, c.1905. She became famous after sinking the German *Cap Trafalgar* during the First World War.

Opposite: Etruria or *Umbria* leaving Liverpool for New York, c. 1890.

Above: Lusitania, the first true superliner, being fitted out at John Brown's, Clydebank.

Left: Mauretania makes her maiden arrival into Liverpool, September 1907.

Lusitania was sunk by the U-boat U20 in May 1915 with the loss of 1,098 lives.

Above: Many of the dead from *Lusitania* were buried in four mass graves in Queenstown.

Below: *Mauretania* had an illustrious war career, serving as an armed merchant cruiser, troopship and as a hospital ship.

After the war, *Mauretania* and *Aquitania* were joined by a third ship, *Berengaria*. *Berengaria* had originally been the German liner *Imperator*. She was sold to Cunard as war reparation for the loss of the *Lusitania*. All three ships were refitted and this was new Cunard trio operated the weekly express service to New York until 1934. The Cunard liners were soon on course to become the darlings of the North Atlantic yet again. The years immediately after the war were a roaring time on the Atlantic. New businesses were being built in war-torn Europe and in America. A flood of emigrants, all seeking a better life, kept the liners full westbound.

It was not to last. In 1920 the USA brought in the Volstead Act which introduced Prohibition – America became a dry nation. This was followed by the Jones Act, limiting immigration to the USA. To combat Prohibition and the lack of emigrant passengers, shipping lines such as Cunard started to run booze cruises. Ships would simply sail out beyond the three mile exclusion limit and open up their bars. Passengers would drink themselves into oblivion and a day or two days later, be disembarcked. This proved to be a good money earner for the non-American shipping lines, especially during the winter season. Cunard used *Berengaria* and *Mauretania* for cruising during this period. With the loss of the very profitable emigrant trade, the shipping lines began to suffer, and no amount of cruises to nowhere could make up for the loss of the lucrative trade.

The 1930s saw the Great Depression, then the threat of another war with Germany, which was re-arming and beginning to annex its eastern neighbours. With its existing fleet all becoming old and outdated, in 1929, Cunard announced construction of a new ship, at 80,000grt she was to be the largest vessel afloat.

Left: Aquitania also served as a troopship and as a hospital ship. Here she is arriving in New York in her dazzle paint camouflage.

Right: Another view of *Mauretania* in her dazzle paint. Designed by Norman Wilkinson, the dazzle scheme was designed to confuse enemy submarines as to the length and direction of travel of the liner.

Right middle: To replace *Lusitania*, the Germans were made to hand over the Hamburg Amerika liner *Imperator* and she became *Berengaria*, Cunard's flagship.

Right bottom: Mauretania was painted overall in white to go cruising in 1932. She was sent to the breaker's yard in 1935.

Below: Aquitania, all 44,500 tons of her, high and dry in Southampton's floating dock in 1925.

Chapter 2

THE CONCEPT OF THE QUEENS

In the late 1920s competition on the high seas was intense. Shipping lines were competing to have the fastest and grandest liners on the North Atlantic to catch the rich and the crème of the immigrant trade. The Cunard liners *Aquitania, Mauretania* and *Berengaria* were still popular, but these ladies were getting old. Competition was coming from the Germans and Italians who were building new ships, and it was rumoured that the French were designing a new superliner which would put all other ships to shame.

Cunard decided to construct a pair of superliners and requests for tenders were sent to every major British shipbuilding yard. These ships should be capable of travelling at 31 knots and operate a weekly service across the Atlantic. Plans were drawn up under secrecy. Naval architects created preliminary designs, sailing schedules and turnaround times were calculated and discussions were made with the ports of New York and Southampton about rebuilding and dredging work that would need to be undertaken to cope with the sheer scale of the new ships.

The contract for the first ship was awarded to John Brown's shipyard on the Clyde on 28 May 1930. The name of the ship was secret, so she was known by her builder's number, Hull 534. She was the biggest man-

made, moving object built in Britain at the time and created her own set of problems. She needed special dry-docking facilities at Southampton because of her size and special insurance as no-one had ever insured anything as large as her before.

Work progressed steadily on the new liner. By November 1931, over 80 per cent of her hull plating was in place and parts were coming from all over Britain for the new liner. She was keeping a nation in work, but as America sank into the Great Depression, it started to affect the rest of the world too. Fortunes collapsed as stocks and shares plunged in value. Only the very rich could still afford to travel, and business for Cunard, like every other shipping line, declined. This slump in business meant that profits turned to losses and, in return, capital projects were put on hold. One of these projects was Hull 534. On 11 December 1931 all work was stopped on the massive liner and Clydebank became another casualty of the Great Depression.

It was not only Clydebank that was affected by the stoppage on the ship, but the whole nation; and one man could see this – Clydebank MP David Kirkwood. He lobbied Parliament and even took his case to the Prince of Wales (later Edward VIII). He was convinced that if work

On account of the Royal arrangements it will be necessary to arrive in the Yard before 2-30 p.m. as the gates will be closed after that time. 2-15 p.m.

CUNARD WHITE STAR LIMITED AND JOHN BROWN & COMPANY, LIMITED

LAUNCH OF S.S. No. 534

from Clydebank Shipyard
on Wednesday, 26th September, 1934,
at 3 p.m.

This Card admits ONE PERSON.

It is to be shewn at Entrance Gate, also on entering the Launching Platform, and given up later on entering Mould Loft, where Tea will be served.

Table M.1   Seat No. 3

NOT TRANSFERABLE

Planning for the new Cunard ship began in 1929. Her name was a secret until her launch in 1934.

Hull 534 became RMS *Queen Mary* and is shown her, photographed by RAF reconnaissance plane, in 1935.

on the liner was restarted, then it would help the economy to recover. The government was wary of getting involved, but eventually agreed to a subsidy and some working capital but only if Cunard merged with the ailing White Star Line.

Many workers returned triumphantly to the shipyard on 3 April 1934. As the hull had been well-cared for during the stoppage, work progressed quickly. On 26 September 1934 Queen Mary launched the liner with a bottle of Australian Chardonnay and the liner was named *Queen Mary* in her honour.

Tugs pulled the *Queen Mary* into the fitting-out basin and work began on installing her engines and interiors. Many famous designers and artists of the day worked on her, including Dame Laura Knight and Doris and Anna Zinkeisen. The new Queen broke away from the 'country house' style of previous Cunard ships and an Art Deco feel was incorporated into the overall interior design of the vessel. Unlike the new French liner *Normandie*, which was Art Deco in the extreme and regarded as the epitome of French chic, *Queen Mary* would be a homely mix of comfort and beautiful design.

In March 1936, *Queen Mary* left her fitting-out basin and sailed for Greenock. Thousands watched from the banks of the Clyde as well as from pleasure steamers.

Queen Mary in the King George V graving dock in early April 1936. The KGV dock was the largest dry dock in the world at the time.

Leaving the UK on 29 August 1936 with her largest compliment of peacetime passengers, *Queen Mary* sailed for New York, War was declared while she was in mid-Atlantic. After a brief sojourn at New York, she was painted grey and turned into a troopship.

The *Queen Mary* left on her maiden voyage on Her Majesty Queen Mary's birthday, 27 May 1936. The ship was full and turned into one class for the voyage. On board Henry Hall and his band played fourteen concerts – the first concerts beamed by radio from a ship. It was truly a momentous occasion.

The *Queen Mary* did not take the Blue Riband on her maiden voyage, because Sir Percy Bates, Chairman of Cunard, preferred the ship to be properly run in before attempting this. But for the next year, the *Queen Mary* and the French Liner *Normandie* tussled for the Blue Riband, and it passed regularly between both ships.

Even before the *Queen Mary* left on her maiden voyage, thoughts turned to her sister. Many of the features of the *Queen Mary* were incorporated into the design of the new ship, but also some improvements had been included too. A Cunard spy was sent on a transatlantic recce on board the new French Liner *Normandie* to report back on any ideas which could be incorporated into the new ship.

In July 1936, the Government gave final confirmation that the monies would be released for the new liner, and on 30 July 1936, it was announced that the new liner would be launched in 1938 and be in service for 1940. The contact between Cunard and John Brown's was signed in October 1936. The new liner was given the yard keel number Hull 552.

Hull 552's keel was laid in December 1936, and this, the main rib of the ship, was completed by January 1937. She was a product of a nation, with parts arriving from all over Britain – Glasgow, Stoke on Trent, Tyneside, Teesside, Basingstoke, Stroud and Derby, to name but a few places.

The launch of Hull 552 took place on 27 September 1938. She was launched by Queen Elizabeth, accompanied by her daughters, the Princesses Elizabeth and Margaret Rose. Immediately before the appointed hour of her launch, Hull 552 decided to take to the water faster than anticipated and began to move. Noticing this, Queen Elizabeth stepped forward and named the ship as it slipped down the ways, crashing a bottle of wine against her hull. She named her *Queen Elizabeth*.

It was the time of the Munich crisis and King George VI was unable to attend – Chamberlain was in Germany and the Nazi regime was threatening Europe with another great war. The uncertainty of the time helped Cunard's business as many people travelled to America to escape the impending war. Just before war was announced, the *Queen Mary* left Britain on 30 August 1939 with 2,332 souls on board. This was the largest amount of passengers she ever carried in peacetime. War was announced four days later on 3 September 1939.

Above left: Queen Elizabeth was still at Clydebank when war was declared but by 1940 it was realised that she would have to move. She sailed down the Clyde on the Spring high tide and made a dash for New York.

Above right: When *Queen Elizabeth* arrived at New York, she joined her sister and the French Line's *Normandie*. For a few days, all three of the world's largest and fastest ships were berthed side by side at New York.

Right: Making her proper maiden voyage in 1946, after a major refit, *Queen Elizabeth* was the biggest ship in the world, while *Queen Mary* was the fastest. A certificate for the maiden voyage.

When the *Queen Mary* arrived in New York, she pulled alongside another great liner *Normandie*. Cunard decided that *Queen Mary* was safer in New York until they could decide what to do with her. On the other side of the Atlantic, her sister *Queen Elizabeth* was still being fitted out. The Admiralty decided that the ship should be fitted out to minimal standards and sent to a safe port, as such a large ship would attract a German bombing raid. So, with the utmost secrecy, *Queen Elizabeth* was fitted out and sent on her way.

On 26 February 1940 at high tide, *Queen Elizabeth* was unceremoniously pulled out of her fitting-out basin by tugs. She made her way down the Clyde to Greenock where a King's Messenger boarded the ship with a special sealed envelope. In this envelope was the ships destination, and

Queen Elizabeth being berthed in Southampton in the late 1950s.

In 1956, the Cunard fleet was still huge. By 1969 almost all of these ships had gone, either sold or scrapped.

it was not to be opened until she was safely at sea. A rumour had been circulating that she was being sent to Southampton – and the rumour was so convincing that German bombers were waiting in Southampton for her arrival! Those of her crew who wanted to disembark were allowed to do so – only to be locked away for a few days until *Queen Elizabeth* was safe.

At sea, Captain Townley opened the orders… her destination New York! The Admiralty had such faith in the shipbuilders that they decided to send an untried and tested ship over 3,500 miles at full speed! *Queen Elizabeth* arrived in New York to the astonishment of the city. Apart from a select few people, no-one knew this giant was on her way, and she caused quite a stir, appearing over the horizon in her battle grey livery!

On 21 March 1940 the *Queen Mary* left New York for Australia to start a new career as a troop carrier. *Queen Elizabeth* then left in October 1940 to follow the *Queen Mary*. Converted into troop carriers, they first ferried troops from Australia to Suez, then the *Elizabeth* took troops from America to Australia. When America entered the war, both Queens were repositioned to take troops from America and Canada to Scotland.

As needs increased, the Queens were transformed from carrying 2,500 troops, to 5,000 troops, increasing to over 15,000 by 1943. The *Queen Mary* still holds the world record for carrying the most number of people

at one time – over 16,000, safely carried through U-boat infested waters at a maximum speed of 30kt.

Mock-ups of both ships were made and training centres were set up at Camp Kilmer to instruct troops how to board and any procedures they may need to know while on the ships. Once on board soldiers were given duties to help out with its smooth running and lectures were given on British culture (many American soldiers did not even know about rationing). The troops were given two meals a day on board and could take as much food as they wanted for lunch, they also shared beds in rotation – as many as three men could be sleeping in the same bed at different times. On the way back to America, the Queens were transformed into floating hospitals and carried casualties home.

After the war was finished, the Queens were used to repatriate hundreds of thousands of troops. The *Mary* took American troops back home, and the *Elizabeth* repatriated Canadian and Commonwealth troops. Then came their most unusual function, the *Mary* and the *Elizabeth* were both turned into giant floating nurseries to take War Brides and their children to their new homes.

On release from War Duties, both the *Queen Mary* and *Queen Elizabeth* were returned to Cunard. The *Elizabeth* was first into service in October 1946. Then the *Mary* joined her in 1947. Cunard had a virtual monopoly on the North Atlantic run as the great liner *Normandie* had succumbed to fire during conversion to a troop carrier in New York in 1940 and many German and Italian liners had been lost as war casualties. Cunard now had the distinction of having the largest liner afloat – the *Elizabeth* – and the fastest – the *Mary*.

For the first time the world could see the splendour of the *Queen Elizabeth*. The *Elizabeth* was designed in the 1930s, but during the 1946 refit, some of her interiors had been updated. Top artists and designers of the time, such as Bainbridge Copnall, Sir Oswald Birley and Jan Juta, all contributed to the interior design and decoration.

The menus on the *Mary* and the *Elizabeth* were as exciting as on the *Mary* prior to the war. Rationing was still in place in Britain, but suppliers in America were able to source foods unavailable in Britain. This impressed travellers very much, but often, unfortunately, their digestive systems did not cope very well with the rich food! The shops on board did a roaring trade too as the clothes on board were not rationed. Excellent service had been part of Cunard's cornerstone, and this returned on both ships. They were *the* place to be seen in the late 1940s and 1950s. The passenger lists read like copies of *Who's Who*. They included film stars, senators, peers, businesspeople, royalty, entertainers and MPs.

Queen Mary leaves Britain for the last time. After 1,001 voyages she was sold to become a tourist attraction in Long Beach, California.

The jet liner had a huge effect on transatlantic travel. This Iberia jet flies over *Queen Mary* in the early 1960s. The aircraft was probably full while the *Queen Mary* was most likely sailing with only a few hundred passengers.

Towards the end of the 1950s, however, Cunard was experiencing challenges with the *Queen Elizabeth* and *Queen Mary*. The first had been the arrival of the SS *United States* in 1952. With much use of lightweight materials, at 52,000grt she was America's answer to Britain's dominance of the waves. *United States* could cruise at 40 knots and easily took the Blue Riband from the *Queen Mary*. *United States* also had the most modern décor – all Formica and aluminium. In fact, the only wood on board was the Steinway piano (because Steinway would not build a piano in aluminium for the ship) and the butcher's block! The second challenge was the arrival of the jet airliner – many people were now choosing to fly the Atlantic in eight to ten hours, rather than spend four days on board a ship. Also, both Queens were getting old – the *Queen Mary* had been in service since 1936, and the *Queen Elizabeth* since 1946 (although she had been a troop carrier during the war since 1940). By the early 1960s, both ships were running at a loss now that most passengers had deserted them for the fashionable jet. At first the Queens were sent cruising. The *Queen Elizabeth* cruised to the Mediterranean and Bermuda, and the *Queen Mary* to the Canaries and Las Palmas. But their sheer size and design were against them. They were too big to be filled to capacity, and they were not designed for hot weather travel – they had no air conditioning or open air pools (although a refit in the mid-1960s saw the *Queen Elizabeth* receive an outdoor pool and air conditioning in her public areas).

These ships were running far below capacity and the decision was taken in these loss-makers had to go and by the late 1960s Cunard had sold the Queens on to other interested parties. The *Queen Mary* was bought by the City of Long Beach in California and was first to retire. After some farewell cruises she left on her final voyage on 31 October 1967, which took her around Cape Horn to the sunny shores of California. There she was made into a hotel, conference centre and tourist attraction – where she remains to this day.

The *Queen Elizabeth*, on the other hand, did not have such an easy life. In April 1968, Cunard announced that the *Queen Elizabeth* had been sold to a consortium of Philadelphia businessmen, who were to relocate her in Delaware, where she would form the centrepiece of a venture incorporating the Seven Wonders of the World, where the *Queen Elizabeth* would be the eighth! Unfortunately, this was not to be and after various futile attempts by the businessmen to keep her – including a move to Port Everglades in Florida – she was eventually auctioned off to a Hong Kong Businessman, Mr C.Y. Tung, who converted her into a floating University – *Seawise University*. Unfortunately, on 9 January 1972, while undergoing refit in Hong Kong harbour, smoke started billowing from her and after many hours ablaze, the hulk of the once great liner keeled over. She remained on her side until cut up for scrap a few years later, but not before taking on a starring role in James Bond's *The Man with the Golden Gun*.

In the late-1950s, when it was thought that the two Queens would be replaced, there were designs made of a new liner which was more suited to the present economic climate… but would she success where the other Queens had failed?

The first attempt, Q3, was not a great success. Cunard was trying to design a large ocean liner comparable with the Queens, but the market at the time required a smaller ocean liner which was suitable for cruising and for line voyages. The Q3 project was eventually shelved, and a smaller dual-purpose ship was designed instead.

The Queen Elizabeth burnt out in Hongkong

Chapter 3

THE LAZY LIZZIE

A new French ocean liner made her maiden voyage in 1962. Her name was *France* and the aim of her owners was that she would become the most stylish and modern liner on the North Atlantic run. She was a new monument to French style and sophistication, designed to be as opulent as the old Normandie, and as *chic*.

Apart from the *France* there were a couple of major reasons why Cunard planned to replace the old Queens. Firstly, numbers of passengers had dwindled since jet aircraft started flying the Atlantic. Instead of four days seasick on a ship, passengers could fly eleven hours by plane. It was faster and more glamorous than these old ships. A new ship was needed to win back some of the passengers from the airlines. Secondly, the Queens were getting old. They were expensive to run and they were designed for the cold North Atlantic run, not for cruising in the tropics. Therefore, there were not easily adaptable to become cruise ships. They had no air conditioning or outside pools (although the *Elizabeth* did have one added during her 1966 refit). They were not cruising ships; their draught was too deep and their length too long for many ports. The Queens were simply not suited to Cunard's needs anymore. Thirdly, the *France* was taking what little trade there was left as

she was modern and adaptable; and if passengers wanted to travel by sea, they did not want to travel by an old-fashioned ship, they wanted a more exciting experience.

All those factors meant that the Queens had to go, before they bankrupted the company.

Q3

Cunard began to look ahead and plan a new ocean liner. The new ship had to be smaller than the present Queens, have the ability to be turned into a cruise ship, and be capable of a speed of almost 30 knots. It was also planned that the new Q3 liner would be about 75,000 tons, carry 2,270 passengers and be about 990ft long, but as time progressed, the costs escalated and it became clear that her operational costs would be too expensive. Therefore the project was shelved and it was back to the drawing board.

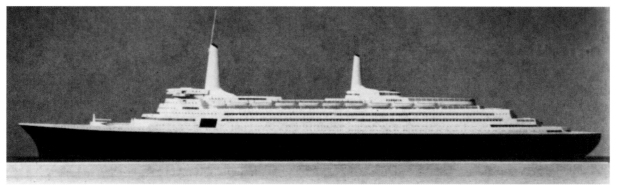

Above left: Q3 never got beyond the design stage before the project was cancelled. A model was made and she does look similar to QE2.

Above right: Sir John Brocklebank, chairman of Cunard and Lord Aberconway sign the contract for Q4 on 30 December 1964.

Below: The design team for Q4 consisted of W. Marcus, F. Wolstenholme, D.N. Wallace and R.P Hutchinson.

Q4

Q4 was a new concept for Cunard. Instead of an ocean liner that just happened to go cruising, Q4 was to be a dual-purpose ship – designed from scratch as an ocean liner and a cruise ship. She had to be both flexible and adaptable to meet the needs of both purposes. The new Cunarder was to be smaller and lighter than the previous Queens. It was predicted that the new ship was to be 58,000 tons, have a passenger capacity of 2,000 passengers and be able to run at 28.5 knots. She was designed to be of a size that she was able to transit the Suez and Panama Canals.

Cunard applied for a loan under the Shipbuilding Credit Scheme. The loan was for £17.6 million and was signed in October 1963.

TWO OR THREE CLASSES?

The first challenge between Cunard's management and the naval architects came as the management insisted on a three-class ship – First, Cabin and Tourist classes. The Naval Architects tried to dissuade them of this as a two-class ship was easier to design and more appropriate for cruising, but Cunard's management was adamant that their market research dictated that this was the passenger preference – it was particularly prevalent to the American market as they preferred a three-class ship. The costs were more and it was not as easy for the naval architects to design a three-class ship, but in the end the management had the final say. A three-class ship it would be.

The best way to find out how to impress and relax new and existing customers was to ask the Cunard Line passengers and crew themselves if they had any views on what would improve life on board for them. As these people were using the facilities every day, the customers and staff knew better than anyone else what would make life easier and more enjoyable. Market research was undertaken amongst the crew and passengers of the *Queen Elizabeth* to find out what improvements could be made to the new Cunarder and some of the suggestions were: business rooms, televisions, teenagers rooms and for the Officers – keeping the deck games away from their quarters. It was even suggested that there was a lack of kennels on the ship as the previous Queens had twenty-four kennels and the new Cunarder would only have eight!

Staff from Cunard were sent to top hotels to examine their modern facilities. The hotels had very few advantages over Cunard ships, except that they tended to use the best equipment and had centralised pantry services for public rooms. The hull was to be built of steel, and the superstructure of aluminium. Aluminium had worked well on the SS *United States* and was much lighter than steel. The weight saving of this aluminium would reduce the liner's running costs at sea. A detailed specification was sent out to many British shipyards so that they could tender for the construction of the new ship.

CONSTRUCTION

In November 1964, four tenders were received from: John Brown's at Clydebank; Swan Hunter & Wigham Richardson, on the Tyne; Vickers Armstrong at Barrow; and Belfast's Harland & Wolff. All tenders came in well over Cunard's estimate and the shipyard with the lowest price and favourable delivery date would not entertain a fixed price contract.

Modifications to the design were made to reduce costs, but still they came in well over estimate. Financing had to be reviewed, but on 30 December 1964, Cunard signed the contract with John Brown Ltd on the Clyde to build the new ship. The estimated delivery date was May 1968 and the contract price was £25,427,000. Cunard had remortgaged five passenger liners and six cargo ships and borrowed extra money from bankers to raise the cash.

The new Cunarder's build number was Hull 736. She was to be built in the same berth (No.4) as her sisters *Mary* and *Elizabeth*. The first keel section was supposed to be laid on 4 July 1965, as this was the traditional date for Cunard Keel Laying Ceremonies – because it was American Independence Day and the anniversary of the day the first Cunard ship *Britannia* left on its maiden voyage. In fact, although the keel was moved a few inches that day, it was actually properly moved several days later because of problems with the concrete blocks which anchored the lifting tackle for the keel.

The superstructure of Hull 736 was welded aluminium. It was light, it resisted corrosion and it was easily welded and fabricated. It had already been used on the SS *United States,* the *Oriana,* the *Canberra* and the *France.* Alcan, the aluminium suppliers, set up a welding school at John Brown's to train the shipyard welders in a new technique which joined the steel hull to the aluminium superstructure.

The hull of 736 had a special shape, determined by her length, breadth and size of her engines. The machinery inside was designed by Tom Kameen, Cunard's technical director, and his team. Instead of having two engine rooms, as with the previous Queens; Hull 736 had one. This allowed more space for public rooms. She had two double reduction geared engines, instead of two single-geared engines as on the previous Queens (which took up double the space). Each produced 55,000 horsepower. Hull 736 also had only three boilers (Foster Wheeler ESDII), instead of the twenty-seven and twelve which the *Mary* and the *Elizabeth* had respectively.

Hull 736's turbines were designed by Pametrada and built by John Brown Engineering (Clydebank) Ltd. They produced a maximum of 310,000lb of steam per hour at 850lb per square inch but the normal output would be 231,000lb. This meant that Hull 736 would use 520 tons of fuel per day – half that of the previous Queens. The new Cunarder had two huge six-bladed propellers. These propellers were made of a special alloy specially chosen to absorb the vibration of the propeller shaft.

Opposite: Testing underway at Clydebank on 2 July 1965, using a model of the hull design for Hull 736.

sea breezes

JANUARY 1969   PRICE 2/6

H Isherwood's
drawings of
Britannia
Persia
Campania
Mauretania
Queen Elizabeth 2

SPECIAL
96 PAGE
CUNARD
ISSUE

Above: Q4 was built on John Brown's No.4 berth, directly opposite the mouth of the river Cart, on the same slipway that had been used to build her two sisters, Queens *Mary* and *Elizabeth*. This view dates from 12 July 1965.

Right: Much of the hull was welded and made up in pre-fabricated sections. This view shows the hull and the internal decks can clearly be distinguished.

Opposite far left: The publicity for the new ship was relentless, with her image appearing everywhere, including in the shipping enthusiast press.

Opposite left: As launch day approached, models of the ship were made to show the design to the world.

Above: A section of her keel, close to the bow, is joined to the rest of the ship.

Right: Q4's bulbous bow is about to be joined to the rest of the ship. Because of the angle for launching, the bow was some thirty-forty feet higher than the stern.

Top: Just some of the 3,000 workers who built Q4 on their way to work. The chap in the bowler hat is one of the works foremen.

Above: Handling upwards of 300 tons of steel a week, the workers were also adept at football too.

Right: Surrounded by scaffolding, the hull of No.736 starts to take shape.

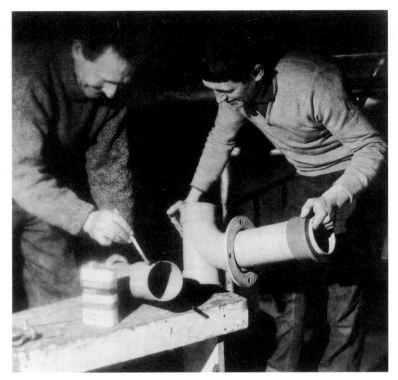

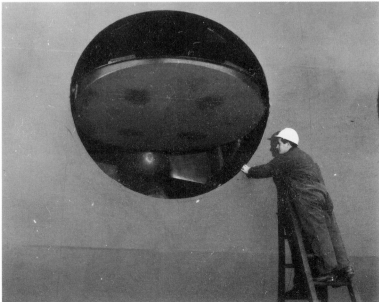

Clockwise from previous page left: A passenger deck, with plumbing already in place.

Assembling plastic piping aboard ship.

Slowly, the open deck starts to become passenger accommodation. Plumbing and wiring is already in place.

Fitting the starboard propeller. It was a tradition at Clydebank to launch larger ships with propellers fitted as there was no local deep draught dry dock large enough for vessels such as Q4. The men give an idea of the sheer size of the six-bladed props.

One of the bow thrusters units, again with a Clydebank worker for scale.

Installing one of the port stabilisers.

With much painting still to be done, the aluminium superstructure starts to take shape.

Launch day looms and the scaffolding for the Royal Box has been erected.

R.M.S. *Carmania*   *Cunard Line*

20th September, 1967

Launching of
R.M.S. Queen Elizabeth II

Captain H. A. Stonehouse, D.S.C.*, R.D.,
R.N.R. (Rtd.)

invites you to partake of a glass of
champagne to toast the new ship.

But what was she to be named. No-one knew, and few guessed. Names like *Queen Victoria* had 5 to 1 odds in local bookmakers, while *Mauretania* had odds of 7 to 2. Very few realised that she would be named after the Queen, although Captain Stonehouse of RMS *Carmania* did manage to get the last part of the name wrong.

20 September 1967 and some half a million people came to watch the launch, lining both banks of the river as well as aboard pleasure steamers moored close by.

THE YACHT

In charge of the exterior design was James Gardner. He was brought in by Cunard as joint design co-ordinator with Dennis Lennon. Gardner's had the idea that 736's exterior should resemble that of a yacht – very sleek and purposeful. Nothing was allowed to clutter her lines and everything above the waterline should take its cue from the Bridge. A ring of concentric circles below the Bridge helped to create this and keep the flow of the lines yacht-like.

The mast leans forward slightly to disguise the fact that it is the same height as the funnel. The terrace decks on the aft end of the ship complete the sweeping lines of a yacht. Curved screens are provided to shield passengers from the weather and assist with the yacht-like appearance.

736's livery was specially designed for her. On previous Cunard ships, the livery had been black and white, or while cruising it had been all-white or all-green liveries. But, breaking away from tradition, Gardner chose a blueish-gray for the hull and white for the superstructure. This reduced the height of the superstructure and stopped the ship looking too top heavy.

Clockwise from right: A sequence of views showing the ship leave the slipway. For a few seconds after the Queen christened her, *Queen Elizabeth 2* remained on the slipway, not moving. 1,400 tons of drag chains helped slow her down as she entered the water.

LAUNCHING

Only four people knew the name of the new liner: Queen Elizabeth herself; Sir Basil Smallpeice, Chairman of Cunard; Sir Michael Adeane, the Queen's Private Secretary and Mr Ronald Senior, Cunard's Deputy Chairman. It had been agreed that the ship would be called *Queen Elizabeth*, as the original *Queen Elizabeth* was out of Cunard service by then. But Queen Elizabeth had other ideas!

When the Queen got up to perform the launch ceremony, a little envelope was handed to her by Mr John Rannie, Managing Director of John Brown Ltd. In it was a card saying "I name this ship, *Queen Elizabeth*"… just in case she forgot the name. But as the Queen named the ship, she changed her mind and called her "*Queen Elizabeth the Second*".

Above right: Despite the drag chains, it took only seventy seconds, with a maximum speed of 22kt, for QE2 to enter her natural environment.

Right: Once launched, and free of her drag chains, *Queen Elizabeth 2* was herded by awaiting tugs into the fitting-out basin and into a mounting controversy over her name.

SCOTTISH DAILY EXPRESS

QUEEN MARY (1934): 81,237 gross tons. 1,019ft. Passengers: 1,948. Speed: 28k.

QUEEN ELIZABETH (1938): 82,997g.t. 1,031ft. Passengers: 2,262. Speed: 28k.

THE Q4 (1967): approx. 58,000 gross tons. 963ft. Passengers: 2,020. Speed: 28k.

Q4

SOUVENIR EDITIONS
September 20|21, 1967

Above: The cover of a souvenir supplement from the *Scottish Daily Express*, designed to contain copies of souvenir issues of the newspaper.

Above right: Before the launch, only a few Cunard officials and Her Majesty knew the name of the new vessel.

Right: Next day, the controversy over the liner's name reigned. Scots were up in arms at the ship's name but Cunard officials neatly got round the problem by saying that the vessel was not named after the reigning monarch (Queen Elizabeth II of England, Queen Elizabeth of Scotland), but after the liner's older, newly retired sister, RMS *Queen Elizabeth*.

SCOTTISH
DAILY EXPRESS

No. 20,931   Wednesday September 20 1967   FOUNDED BY LORD BEAVERBROOK   Weather: Showers

Q4 name flashed to Balmoral
THE QUEEN IN THE KNOW

Queen's view of Q4 from royal dais . . . this was scene yesterday

SCOTTISH
DAILY EXPRESS

No. 20,932   Thursday September 21 1967   FOUNDED BY LORD BEAVERBROOK   Weather: Sunny periods   Price 4d

QE
SOUVEN
BIG PAGES
BIG PICTU

Surprised Scots protest at her name

Q.E. 2 HITS FIRST SQUALL

THE OTHER CHOICES WERE MARGARET AND ANNE

By JACK McGILL

THOUSANDS of Scots were disappointed yesterday at the choice of name for the new Cunarder.

They called the name, Queen Elizabeth II, "unimaginative," "thoughtless," and "pretentious"

Left and below left: For over a year, fitting out continued, and QE2 slowly began to resemble an ocean greyhound. These two views show her soon before her tortuous journey down the shallow and twisting River Clyde towards the open sea at Greenock.

Left: QE2's funnel looks dramatic from any angle.

A VERY DISTINCTIVE FUNNEL

A sleek yacht should have a sleek funnel… and for Hull 736 a conventional funnel was never part of the concept. The funnel is used for pushing the engine and gas emissions high enough so that the emissions disappear into the atmosphere without falling back onto the ship and covering passengers with specks of dust and soot. This should have been a fairly simple task, but designing a funnel that can push emissions that high is actually quite difficult. In the past, devices such as mortar-board tops, or domed stacks have been used on top of the funnel to make sure that the wind direction is best for pushing the emissions away from the decks. But these methods provide no guarantee that the smoke and gas would not be blown back to cover passengers sitting on deck.

Instead on Hull 736, the smoke plume streams out horizontally behind the funnel, and the base of the plume is parallel to the waterline. This means the emissions stay above the decks until it is out at sea. The design for this funnel incorporates a scoop-shaped base that sweeps the air up and carries all the gasses upwards. However, the stack creates a vacuum which pulls the gasses down, but an extremely large vent behind the stack pushes out engine and boiler room air to equalise the vacuum and keep the air pressure moving so the horizontal stream of the smoke plume remains.

The design for the funnel became known as 'The Boot' because it had the main stack (which looked like a leg) and a shield around the side to deflect the wind up and behind the vents (the sides and back of a boot). The air vent became the focus of the funnel and this was emphasised by making it as high as possible. The funnel was painted the distinctive Cunard red and the surrounds white.

A very modern funnel for a very modern ship…

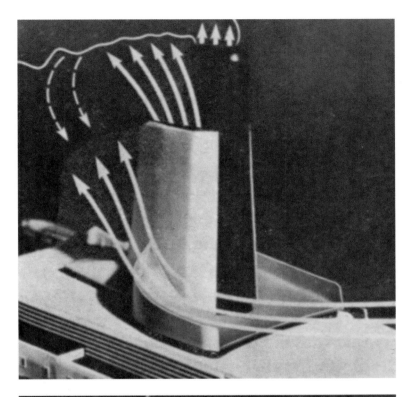

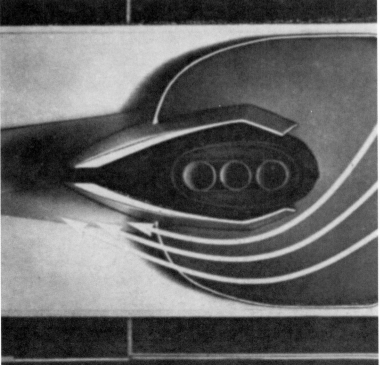

Most people did not mind this, the Americans loved it, but the Scottish were upset. In Scotland, Queen Elizabeth is only Queen Elizabeth the First because the English Queen Elizabeth the First was on the throne before Scotland and England became united; therefore the English Queen Elizabeth the Second is Scotland's Queen Elizabeth the First. The Scottish National Party was in an uproar, saying that it was an insult to the people who built her. But Cunard passed this off by saying that she was the Second *Queen Elizabeth* ocean liner, and indeed this is why she has a numeral 2 rather than the more traditional 'II' suffix.

The launch took place on 20 September 1967 at 2.30pm. The new *Queen Elizabeth 2* took seventy seconds from the time the bottle hit her hull to entering the Clyde after hurtling down the slipway at 22 miles per hour. Because of this seventy second gap, the *Daily Telegraph* named her 'The Lazy Lizzie'. The ship, which was to travel the world representing Britain, was unceremoniously dragged into her fitting-out basin to have her engines, running gear and sumptuous interiors fitted.

Queen Elizabeth 2
Maiden Cruises aboard the QE2

From New York   February - March 1969

Port	Arrive	Depart		Port	Arrive	Depart

February 1st, 1969. 12 days.
$550.

*New York		Sat Feb 1 pm
Curacao	Wed Feb 5 am	Thu Feb 6 am
Barbados	Fri Feb 7 am	Sat Feb 8 am
Martinique	Sat Feb 8 am	Sun Feb 9 am
St. Thomas	Mon Feb 10 am	Tue Feb 11 am
New York	Thu Feb 13 am	

February 14th, 1969. 14 days.
$645.

**New York		Fri Feb 14 pm
St. Thomas	Mon Feb 17 am	Mon Feb 17 pm
Martinique	Wed Feb 19 am	Thu Feb 20 am
Barbados	Thu Feb 20 am	Fri Feb 21 am
Curacao	Sat Feb 22 am	Sun Feb 23 am
Cristobal	Mon Feb 24 am	Mon Feb 24 pm
New York	Fri Feb 28 am	

March 1st, 1969. 9 days.
$415.

**New York		Sat Mar 1 pm
Barbados	Wed Mar 5 am	Thu Mar 6 am
Martinique	Thu Mar 6 am	Thu Mar 6 am
St. Thomas	Fri Mar 7 am	Fri Mar 7 pm
New York	Mon Mar 10 am	

Easter cruise from Southampton
14 day cruise

De luxe class from £375
Cruise class from £195

Port	Arrive	Depart
Southampton		Thu Apr 3 pm
Tangier	Sat Apr 5 am	Sat Apr 5 pm
Athens	Tue Apr 8 am	Wed Apr 9 am
Malta	Thu Apr 10 am	Thu Apr 10 pm
Naples	Fri Apr 11 am	Sat Apr 12 pm
Gibraltar	Mon Apr 14 am	Mon Apr 14 pm
Lisbon	Tue Apr 15 am	Tue Apr 15 pm
Southampton		
	Thu Apr 17 am	

*Embarkation 8.30 am–10.30 am
**Embarkation 1 pm–4.30 pm
Sails from Pier 92, North River, New York, N.Y.

Above: After a maiden voyage to New York, cruises to the Caribbean were planned.

Right: Her preview cruise was to be on 10 January 1969, but problems with her turbines put paid to her initial maiden voyage in the spring of that year. The cheapest fare for her preview cruise was £98.

Opposite above: A rare view of her stern, taken on 14 September 1968, as work continues apace on her accommodation.

Opposite below: Bedecked in lights, steam coming from her funnel, the engines are tested prior to her first journey under her own power, from Clydebank to Greenock.

QUEEN ELIZABETH 2   PREVIEW CRUISE   10 JANUARY 1969

ONE DECK

	Fares per suite £
De luxe suites with bedroom (2 beds), sitting room, 2 baths, showers and toilets	876

Outside rooms with bath, shower and toilet

	Fares per adult £
Suite rooms, with two beds - 1034,1036,1037,1038,1039,1040,1041,1042,1043,1044, 1045,1046,1047,1048,1049,1050,1051,1052,1053,1054, 1055,1057	219
With two beds - 1026,1028,1029,1030,1031,1033,1060,1062,1063,1064, 1065,1066,1067,1069	199
With two beds - 1001,1008,1009,1016,1018,1019,1020,1021,1022,1023, 1024,1025,1027,1068,1070,1071,1072,1073,1074,1075, 1076,1077,1079,1088,1090,1091,1093	193
∮With two beds - 1002,1003,1012,1015,1078,1081,1102,1103	187
With two beds - 1104,1105,1110,1111,1114,1115,1118,1119,1120,1121	158
With three beds - 1106,1107,1116,1117	146
Single bedrooms - 1006,1007,1014,1017,1058,1061,1082,1085,1092,1094, 1095,1096,1097,1099	216
Single bedrooms - 1032,1035,1056,1059,1084,1086,1087,1089	210

Inside rooms with shower and toilet

Single bedrooms - 1100,1108,1109,1112,1113	160

TWO DECK

	Fares per suite £
De luxe suites with bedroom (2 beds), sitting room, 2 baths, showers and toilets	796

Outside rooms with bath, shower and toilet

	Fares per adult £
Suite rooms, with two beds - 2065,2066,2067,2068,2069,2071,2072,2073,2074,2075, 2076,2077,2078,2079,2080,2081,2082,2083,2084,2085, 2086,2088,2090,2092	199
With two beds - 2091,2093,2095,2097,2098,2100,2102,2104	174
With two beds - 2040,2041,2042,2043,2044,2045,2046,2047,2054,2055, 2056,2057,2058,2059,2060,2061,2062,2064,2099,2101, 2106,2108,2109,2111,2116,2117,2118,2119,2124,2126	168
∮With two beds - 2050,2051,2105,2112	168
With two beds - 2121,2127,2131,2132,2133,2136,2138,2141,2142,2144, 2145,2147,2150,2152	146
Single bedrooms - 2036,2037,2038,2039,2052,2053,2089,2096,2107,2114	198
Single bedrooms - 2034,2035,2063,2070,2087,2094,2113,2115,2120,2122	192

Outside rooms with shower and toilet

With two beds - 2004,2016,2017,2018,2019,2026,2027,2028,2029,2125, 2128,2139	137
With three beds - 2123	133
Single bedrooms - 2001,2003,2007,2008,2011,2012,2020,2021	160

∮Rooms with small rooms adjoining in which bed and pullman may be fitted at minimum fares.

Above: Two workers walk under her lifeboat davits, either at Clydebank or at Southampton.

Right: By 26 March 1969, QE2 was safely berthed in the King George V graving dock at Southampton after successful turbine and sea trials. Her hull was then cleaned in preparation for her delayed maiden voyage.

Opposite, clockwise from top left: These first voyage were not to be, and QE2 was sent back to be fixed by her builders. These views show QE2 on her sea trials and her clean lines can be appreciated from these early views of her on the flying mile speed trials.

Chapter 4

A FLOATING RESORT

Squirrels are normally little cute, furry creatures with big tails that climb trees… But during the fitting out of the new *Queen Elizabeth 2* squirrels became a major problem, but these squirrels had two legs and wore clothes! Squirreling was the art of stealing from a ship in order to keep the ship in the shipyard longer; this in turn keeping men in employment for longer. There was also the advantage that furnishings could be 'acquired' for houses and flats. In fact, there was a flourishing market around Glasgow with items bearing the *QE2* logo. Lifeboats had been stripped, houses filled with items of furniture from the ship, lavatories refitted with new toilet bowls and there was very little anyone did to stop this sharp practice. In fact, even the blue paint for her hull was in demand in Glasgow and Clydebank pubs. The new *Queen Elizabeth 2* was certainly not the first ship to be 'squirreled' and was certainly not the last! As a result of all this squirreling, there were some very stylish properties in Clydebank's tenements.

QE2's interior fixtures and fittings were very modern. Like past Cunarders, the *QE2* reflected the styles and tastes of the time. Unlike past Cunarders, where the décor was distinctly in the style of a grand hotel and not a ship, the design of the new *QE2* acknowledged that she was a ship,

and a big one at that. The late sixties were the time of psychedelia; of rich mixtures of opposing colours and *QE2*'s interior design was influenced by social events of the time, especially the 'Space Age', with the recent Apollo missions and the imminent event of man's first steps on the moon.

Unlike Cunard passenger ships of the past, the new *Queen Elizabeth 2* had to have some interior changes for her dual-purpose role. These were made at the construction stage and were fully integrated into the ship. One of the first innovations was air-conditioning throughout the ship, then there were to be outdoor as well as indoor swimming pools. Private showers and toilets were a must, and a lido deck and nightclub were seen as essentials.

Originally an internal committee had been appointed by Cunard in the early 1960s to look at interior design of the new liner, including Lady Brocklebank (the wife of the company's chairman), Mr Anthony Hume (vice-chairman of Cunard) and Dan Wallace (Naval Architect). They spent two years travelling to hotels and liners all over Britain, Europe and America to evaluate what travellers preferred in interior design. Lady Brocklebank was well aware that interior designers are apt to forget that they are designing for travellers, and while a design might look aesthetically pleasing, it may not be practical for the type of traveller accommodated there.

Right: Leaving Southampton on her maiden voyage, QE2 is viewed by thousands of sightseers, and numerous television crews, such as the Southern team in the Ford Transit van at bottom left.

Below: Her triumphant arrival in New York was no different, with thousands viewing the arrival, and television crews ready to interview her lucky passengers.

However, in 1966, Sir John Brocklebank, Chairman of Cunard, resigned due to ill health, and Sir Basil Smallpeice replaced him. Sir Basil had new modern ideas about the design of the ship. Firstly, the new ship would be a luxurious hotel that had transportation added; secondly the idea of separate classes was not acceptable – a variety of accommodation would be offered and the public spaces used by all passengers. Thirdly, Sir Basil wanted the new ship to be part of the holidaying experience. The number of public rooms could be cut and rooms could be amalgamated to take more people. The new design team consisted of Sir Duncan Oppenheim, Chairman of the Council of Industrial Design, James Gardner (exterior design) and Dennis Lennon (interior design) as joint design co-ordinators and Dan Wallace, Naval Architect.

Dennis Lennon's team had originally been working on the Columbia Restaurant, the Grill Room, the Library and Theatre Bar. When Dennis Lennon took on the overall interior design he wanted the interior of the whole ship to be designed as a whole, rather than a series of individual projects. This would mean that the ship would develop a character of her own. Lennon then took the designers to places he admired to let them get a feel for what he was aiming for – a modern, elegant background with designs reflecting the best of contemporary thought and manufacture; in other words, a floating resort.

While *QE2* has been refitted many times since she came into service, some vestiges of the original design remain to this day, most notably in the Queen's Room and the Library.

Design magazine and the *Architect's Journal* both devoted an issue each to the new liner, such was her importance in art and design circles.

According to *Design* magazine, the signal decks had 'strong structural forms'.

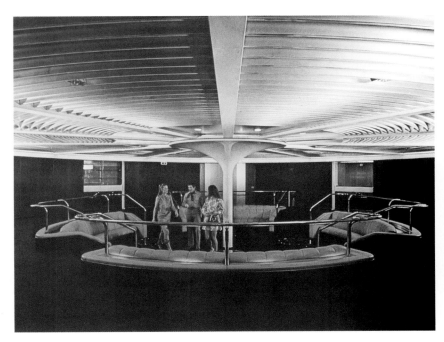

Above: On two deck was the midships lobby, where passengers would enter the ship for the first time.

Right: The four main staircases had different coloured rails and panels to help orientation aboard the huge vessel.

MIDSHIPS LOBBY

Deck Two, Midships: Designed by Dennis Lennon, this was (and still is) the first area most passengers saw as the entered the ship. Sunken green settees made from hide formed a circle while a central white column of GRP mushroomed up towards the white ceiling. The walls were painted dark with an ink blue carpet.

Above and above right: Jan Bannenberg's Double Room was the largest interior room of any passenger ship to date.

Right: The Columbia Restaurant was in sober colours of brown, gold and apricot.

Left: The restaurant chairs were designed by Robert Heritage and were made by Race. They were upholstered in red and white in the Britannia Restaurant and brown in the Columbia Restaurant.

DOUBLE ROOM

Upper and Boat Decks, aft: Australian Jan Bannenberg was the designer of the famous Double Room. It was the largest room on the ship. The room served many purposes: coffee lounge, dancing room, venue for special occasions and entertainment. The room was two decks high and the upper deck was balconied. The centre of the room had a dance floor with a stair rising up from one end and a circular sepia-tinted enclosure for the band at the other end. To sit on there were William Plunkett-designed *Kingston* chairs and settees. These were in red, orange and puce, and on the floor was herringbone carpet of damson and puce, woven by Kosset Carpets.

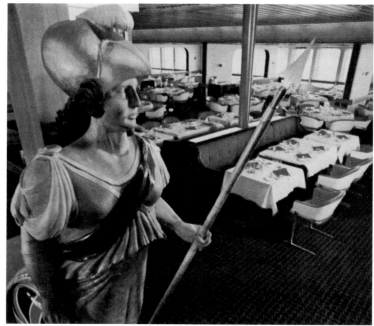

Right: The hard-wearing Steelite china was manufactured by Ridgeway Potteries, and was manufactured after seven year's research.

Left and below: Dennis Lennon designed the Upper Deck library, with beige and blue being the predominant colours in the room.

RESTAURANTS

Both the Britannia and the Columbia Restaurants were served off the same kitchen, making for ease of use.

Britannia, *Upper Deck, forward:* Designer Dennis Lennon chose a red, white and blue colour scheme with screens of oak-veneered duck-boarding to break down the space into intimate dining areas. This restaurant seated 800 and the colour scheme was used to create a lively atmosphere. Instead of giving the new Cunarder a silver rose bowl like its predecessors, Lloyds of London presented the new ship with a Britannia Figurehead, which was mounted just inside the main entrance of the restaurant. The banquette seating was in blue, while the chairs were in bright red and white. The carpet produced by the Carpet Manufacturing Company was blue with a black trefoil pattern.

Columbia, *Quarter Deck, Midships:* Also designed by Dennis Lennon. The theme of this room was glamour. Panels of bronze-tinted glass divided the room and a donkey-brown coloured carpet made by Kosset adorned the floor. The restaurant sat 500 people across the width of the ship. Leather wall panels and Race chairs helped to set the mood.

LIBRARY

Upper Deck, Midships: Beige and blue were the predominant colours in Dennis Lennon's library. The library was divided into bays, the largest of which housed the librarian's desk and floor to ceiling bookshelves. The furniture in the library consisted of R.S. Stevens *Discus* chairs, rosewood tables, and Bernat Klein armchairs upholstered in blue and green checks. Additionally there were blue Perspex column reading lamps bolted to the walls and tables. There was a beige carpet which is common to both the library and the Theatre Bar.

Above and below: With a view of the bows, the Lookout was a dramatic room, still used as a bar to this day.

Left: Also designed by Lennon was the Theatre Bar.

THEATRE BAR

Upper Deck, Midships: In common with the library, the Theatre Bar had a beige carpet running through it. Facing the passenger, as they entered from the Promenade, was a bright red GRP wall with an egg-crate pattern. A bright red piano, William Plunkett tables and chairs, and also red Bertoia chairs complemented the mushroom-shaped lamps by Artemide.

THE LOOKOUT

Upper Deck, forward: This room, overlooking the bows of the ship, was designed by Theo Crosby. It is a narrow kidney-shaped room stretching the width of the ship. A vast irregular screen of stainless steel and bronze vertical bars lined the back wall (designed by Gillian Wise). The club-like atmosphere of The Lookout still emits a sober atmosphere. The furniture was designed by Crosby/Fletcher/Forbes and made of GRP and black *Cirrus* upholstery, the carpet was green, panelled walls in cedar of Lebanon veneer and the only touch of real colour was a bright red microfilm chart reader showing charts of the locations the ship was travelling in.

Above left: Finishing work being undertaken in the Queen's Room.

Above right: Almost square in shape, at 105x100ft, the Queen's Room is a dramatic venue. Originally, with a light, airy look, this room now looks much darker after numerous refits and minor redesigns.

THE QUEEN'S ROOM

Quarter Deck, aft: The room is almost square – 105ft by 100ft; but the designer Michael Inchbald used a number of techniques to give the impression that the room was longer and higher than it was.

The ceiling is open perforated, white glass-fibre-reinforced plastics, lit from behind. The duct casings are disguised as thin columns with trumpets towards the ceiling, appearing round, but are actually oval in shape. The walls at each end deceive the eye by making the width appear smaller by mixing walnut-veneered GRP with mirrors. The main colour in the room was white. There were white plastic Lurashell chairs made in two sizes and upholstered with Connolly leather. The walnut-topped Arkana tables had trumpeted bases at the bottom. The carpet was honey and pale beige, woven by Thomson Shepherd. It was 80 per cent wool and 20 per cent nylon. The room was slightly sunken and the sofas around the plant stands were covered with red tweed upholstery by the Donald Brothers. At one end of this sunken area was a bandstand. Inchbald projected some interest into this area by making the area at the back of the bandstand white and using an array of coloured, moving lights to highlight the band.

INDOOR POOLS

Various areas around the ship: As built *QE2* had four swimming pools – two outdoor and two indoor. Jon Bannenberg designed the pool on Deck Six. The tiles were natural-coloured Dorset stone and the walls had a finish of Glamorock aggregate. The pool had a double row of cylindrical changing rooms in brilliant vermilion, glass-reinforced plastics. The insides of these cubicals were linked with pink Indian cotton similar to the curtains and they had GRP walls – some cubicles were fitted with showers. Adjoining the pool was the Turkish bath area in a similar colour scheme.

The other indoor pool on Deck Seven was designed by Dennis Lennon in yellow and white. There was a Sauna and rest area leading off it. The equipment and furniture for this area was supplied by Rantasalmi of Finland.

THEATRE

Upper Deck, Midships: With a seating capacity of 530, this room had a multi-functional capacity – conference hall, lecture theatre, cinema, and church. The interior was purposefully designed to reflect as much of the sound as possible. GRP panels adorn the ceilings and walls and these are painted stone white. The theatre is finished with a Wilton carpet. There are four glass-fronted interpreters' booths and a projectionist's area. These have slatted screens which can cover them. Gaby Schreiber & Associates-designed seats in plum and puce adorned the theatre.

Above left: The glass fibre surrounds to the windows on the promenade deck were made by Glasdon.

Above right: Designed by Stefan Buzas and Alan Irvine, the 736 Club had a discotheque installed.

736 CLUB

Boat Deck, midway between forward and midships: Named after the Hull Number of *Queen Elizabeth 2*, the 736 Club was designed by Stefan Buzas and Alan Irvine as the ship's nightclub. It comprised three main elements – bar, dance floor and sitting areas. The dance floor was sunken and surrounded by lattice-work screens (not unlike the Mackintosh Screens used in the Cranston Tearooms). These were surrounded by semi-circular banquette seating, tables and Bertoia Chairs, upholstered in brown. The exclusive atmosphere was further emphasised by the use of timber, leather and Wilton carpet in rich blue. All the working surfaces were covered in Indian laurel wood. In one of the semi-circular booths a discotheque was installed. The disco equipment had been adapted to incorporate the mood lighting on the dance floor. This room was not part of Cunard's original plan but it proved successful as a bar and discotheque during the day and a Club (where hot snacks were served) in the evening.

GRILL ROOM

Quarter Deck, midway between forward and midships: This was the equivalent of the Verandah Grill on the old Queens. Seating 100 guests, this restaurant had a cover charge and there was a spiral staircase linking the restaurant with a small bar below. Dennis Lennon's idea was to create a restaurant with a rich atmosphere. It had plum velvet panelling on the walls, silver aluminium on the ceiling, oyster-covered silk curtains. The table were covered in pink cloths and the seats covered in plum leather. There were statues in the four corners representing the Four Elements. These were by Janine Jane, and stood about 5ft high.

Q4 ROOM

Quarter Deck, aft: Designed by David Hicks, this was another dual-purpose room – bar in the daytime, nightclub in the evening. Four screens split this room up. The walls were covered in men's suiting material, with panels of bright chromium edging, and in between the panels he used gold leaf. The red carpet had grey, blue and white geometric patterns, and Hick used Perspex and Polaroid glass to accentuate parts of the room. The furniture comprised of black fabric chairs with black fabric cloths, although during daytime the tablecloths were changed to pink and red.

SHOPPING ARCADE

Boat Deck, midships: Like the 736 Club, the shopping arcade was designed by Stefan Buzas and Alan Irvine. The shops were along the seaboard side of the upper section of the Double Room. The rooms were 22ft wide by 8ft deep and designed to fit between the ship's bulkheads. The shops had illuminated display cases to either side of the service counter which had a bonded storeroom underneath.

TEENAGE AREA/CHILDREN'S PLAY AREAS

Children's Area, *Sports Deck, midships:* The Children's area was a large rectangular room, broken up by curving orange and white GRP screens. These are large enough to give children privacy to play, but small enough for the nursery nurses to see over them. The furniture consisted of large BXL plastic cubes in bright colours. These could be used as stools or building blocks. The Children's area also boasted an enclosed veranda, a playpool and a climbing frame. Galt Toys supplied some of the play equipment on board.

Teenage Area, *Boat Deck, midships:* This room was designed by students from the Royal College of Art. Two students, Elizabeth Mower White and Tony Heaton, were chosen by Lady Casson, head of interior design.

Right: Perspex screens by Rory McEwen for QE2's night club.

Below: The children's play area was divided into separate cubby holes.

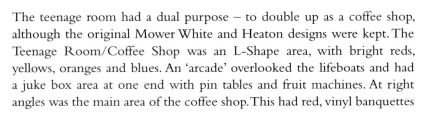

The teenage room had a dual purpose – to double up as a coffee shop, although the original Mower White and Heaton designs were kept. The Teenage Room/Coffee Shop was an L-Shape area, with bright reds, yellows, oranges and blues. An 'arcade' overlooked the lifeboats and had a juke box area at one end with pin tables and fruit machines. At right angles was the main area of the coffee shop. This had red, vinyl banquettes in booths with brown Formica-topped tables with a black perimeter line. The booth walls were lined with brown Hessian. The central area had a Hypalon floor with a huge black and brown bullseye.

SYNAGOGUE

Three Deck, forward: Cunard consulted Professor Mischa Black and asked him if the synagogue from the *Queen Mary* could not be transferred and used on the new *Queen Elizabeth 2*. Unfortunately, his reply was that this was not in keeping with modern Jewish trends, so a new one was designed.

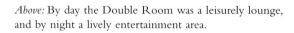

Above: By day the Double Room was a leisurely lounge, and by night a lively entertainment area.

Top, above right: The Columbia Restaurant had space for 500 diners at each sitting.

Right: The red and white chairs of the Britannia restaurant were very distinctive.

Above and above right: With seating for only one hundred, the Grill Room was a much more sedate and intimate dining area.

Right: The Midships Bar was located next to the Columbia Restaurant. It was furnished in green leather and mohair velvet.

Above, left and right: The turbo-alternators, boilers and auxiliary machinery were controlled from the main control room, behind which was located the computer room.

Right: The computer controlled the ship's machinery and the safety control panel controlled the fire precautions.

Above left: The Quarter Deck Pool and Lido. There was over 6,000sq.ft of deck space on QE2 as originally built.

Above right: Every cabin was air-conditioned and had a six channel radio for in-room entertainment.

Left: In her unique livery, QE2 was, and still, is a majestic sight when approaching or leaving by tender.

PASSENGER ACCOMMODATION

LUXURY SUITES

There were five different colour schemes in the fifty-four first class suites – cream, blue, sage, olive green and chestnut. The timber veneers were in cedar, ash and rosewood and were used on the walls. The designers were Dennis Lennon, Gaby Schreiber and Buzas and Irvine. Each suite consisted of a sleeping/living room, bathroom, entrance hall, dressing room and a closet. All cabins had air-conditioning, telephone and radios. When a suite bedroom was converted to a living room, the beds could be converted to settees. In the bedrooms, two single beds were pushed together to make a double. The cabin furniture materials were designed to have the minimum amount of care and at the same time maintain their freshness.

FIRST-CLASS

Yellow ochre, pale blue and white, orange, and red were the colours chosen by Jon Bannenberg for the first-class cabins. These cabins all had built-in furniture of wood veneers and Formica. Each cabin was furnished with Hille Nimbus chairs and Arkana tables and stools. Some of the cabins had interlinking doors allowing two cabins to be converted into a suite. The cabins also had an unusually high amount of storage space including a large walk-in wardrobe, large enough to store trunks; and drawer space running the width of the cabin underneath the window.

TOURIST-CLASS

These cabins were smaller than the first-class cabins, but were by no means inferior. Designed mostly in white, they incorporated different colour schemes to give them a sense of individuality. These colour schemes are: yellow and gold, white and black, blue and green, pink and either orange or red, and brown and yellow. The mirror panel above the headboard hid the electrical wiring and on its black Formica base were the controls for the radio, lights, service and television (this was envisaged when the ship was built but not installed until much later). The panel took the combined efforts of Tannoy, Rediffusion, and Midland Electrical

Right, above and below: There were four swimming pools aboard, two inside and two outside pools, as well as a huge expanse of deck area.

Manufacturing to produce and was an imaginative and forward-thinking piece of equipment.

In addition to the standard rooms, *Queen Elizabeth 2* also included 106 rooms for single travellers as it was envisaged that the ship might attract a high proportion of single clientele. There were also specially adapted rooms for wheelchair users. The bathroom doors would be at least 26in wide, and there was extra space in the toilet to allow a wheelchair to manoeuvre. A suggestion of having small ramps was also made to allow the wheelchair users to gain access to areas on different levels. *QE2* was the first liner to incorporate wheelchair adaptations.

ROOMS NEVER USED

While almost every eventuality was thought of, there were a couple of rooms which were deemed unsuitable: while Cunard provided a secretarial service on board *QE2*, it was considered a step too far to include a stock exchange because immediate ship to shore information technology was still in its infancy. This was despite the fact that Cunard's *Berengaria* had a stock exchange facility installed in the late 1920s.

Another room that got no further than the planning stage was a discotheque. Helen Cordet, who ran the London Saddle Room, was interested in running this area, but negotiations fell through. The idea was to appeal to the American market by decorating it in the style of the English hunting stables.

Dennis Lennon, responsible for the overall design of the interior with specific responsibility for the main restaurants and the Midships Bar.

James Gardner, who had responsibility for the exterior styling of QE2.

Originally the Q4 room was to be the ship's casino but this idea was dropped when it was realised that the whole casino would need to be dismantled before the ship arrived at a US port. For a ship making regular transatlantic voyages to New York, the inconvenience would have ben horrendous.

GRAPHIC DESIGN

The graphic design throughout the ship was given to Theo Crosby of Crosby, Fletcher, Forbes. The design was carried through from the menus to the notices in the bathroom. The distinctive 'Cunard' and 'QE2' logos were instantly recognisable and very quickly became synonymous with *Queen Elizabeth 2*.

BRONZE GLASS DOORS

Each of the bronze-glass doors aboard ship weighed 1.5cwt – which, considering weight is a big issue on board a ship, was very heavy. Imported from the United States and made of Parallelo glass, there were more than their toll on the china stocks. During one voyage at the start of her career, when *Queen Mary* hit a storm over 36,000 pieces of crockery were lost.

The new *QE2* china also had to be stackable and interlockable, as space is at a premium on board ship. It also meant that the china was less likely to move and break during a storm.

Ridgeway Potteries, part of the Allied English Potteries group, won the contract to supply the tableware on the new liner. They had been developing a new type of 'unbreakable china' called Steelite. In tests carried out by Ridgeway, Steelite performed very well in a factory canteen – only a handful of pieces were broken or cracked. The only difference made to the design of Steelite on board *QE2* was that the edges of the plates had to be thicker than usual tableware in order to cushion the blow of other tableware as the ship rolled in bad weather. However, it was also added that the cups and saucers should be made of bone china, as it was more elegant to drink from than the much thicker Steelite ones.

Even though there were different classes on the ship, Cunard decided that all classes should use the same plates. This cut down on expense. Under the watchful eye of the Marquis of Queensbury, Julia Chandler was assigned to create the decoration around the china. Ridgeway recommended an under-glaze to their Steelite tableware as the pattern would be more robust, but as Cunard wanted to use a gold glaze, then this

Stefan Buzas, along with Alan Irvine, designed the 736 Club, the shops and the boat deck gallery.

thirty pairs of these doors on board with a combined total weight of around 5 tons. Each door is 7 ft high by 3 ft wide. The toughened bronze glass is half an inch thick.

Vertically, a strip of leather runs down the door, and also a strip runs across the door to meet the push handle. The colour of this leather relates closely to the room it opens into. The colours used are black, beige, green, plum, blue, brown and red.

TABLEWARE

The Marquis of Queensbury of the Royal College of Art was given responsibility for designing and rationalisation of the tableware. On the *Queen Mary*, *Queen Elizabeth* and other Cunard liners of the time there were up to ninety different pieces of tableware carried. This was deemed too much. Instead it was considered that twenty-four pieces of tableware would be enough.

The new tableware had to be robust – any china travelling by ship had to be, as years of going through steam dishwashers and storms could take

Lord Queensberry was consultant to Cunard for the QE2's tableware.

Michael Inchbald designed the Queen's Room and the Quarter Deck Library.

Responsible for designing the largest room afloat was the Australian Jon Bannenberg.

could not be, as Steelite under-glazing would accept any colour except for gold. So Julia Chandler's on-glaze gold design would become the standard pattern for the new liner.

GLASSES, CUTLERY AND SILVERWARE

The Steelite was complemented by specially designed glasses, cutlery and silverware. The silverware was by Eric Clements and was in silver plate. David Mellor designed the cutlery which was made by Elkington. A range of twenty-one glasses, tumblers, jugs and carafes were made by Waterford Glass.

The branding and image that the new Cunarder portrayed before her launch would stay with her for life – it was essential that the image was of luxury. This was true not only of her furniture, but also had to be carried through her fittings and even down to the tableware. Only the best would do!

The *Queen Elizabeth 2* was, like her eldest sister *Queen Mary*, yet another ship which brought together a nation. Her steel came from Glasgow, fibreglass came from Northumberland; her closed circuit television came from Berkshire and stabilisers from Edinburgh. Turbines came from Rochdale, fire extinguishers from Middlesex and mirrors from Rugby. She was truly a flag-ship for a nation!

Chapter 5

PEACE... AND WAR

This new liner, the *Queen Elizabeth 2*, would have four official maiden voyages. The first would be on 10 January 1969, which would consist of four days cruising wherever the Captain wanted to go; the second would be a 13 day trip to New York taking in the Canaries and Caribbean starting on 17 January; the third being her return transatlantic crossing from New York on 11 March; and her fourth would be on 3 April, a Mediterranean cruise from Southampton.

Even before *Queen Elizabeth 2* left the fitting-out basin, plans were afoot to run a weekly transatlantic service using Compagnie Generale Transatlantique's (CGT) SS *France* and Cunard's *Queen Elizabeth 2*. It made sense because both Cunard and CGT had one ship each and it was impossible for either to maintain a weekly service on their own. A combined effort by the two companies would ensure a scheduled transatlantic presence on the Atlantic for those who preferred not to travel by jet. Passengers also gained a huge benefit – they were able to travel on two very different, but equally as glamorous, liners.

By the end of 1968, Cunard was a rather protracted version of the company it once was. The Line had been making heavy losses because many more passengers now flew the Atlantic rather than sailing it. Only two passenger ships were left in service; *Carmania* and *Franconia*. Both the Queens had been sold as had all of the other loss-making vessels. The head offices of Cunard were also moved from Liverpool to London, and staff redundancies were made.

One bright spot on the horizon was that Prince Charles had agreed to visit the new *Queen Elizabeth 2*. His visit coincided with *QE2* leaving John Brown's to go down the Clyde for her sea-trials. First he was given a guided tour of the nation's new flagship (avoiding the unfinished sections), then he sailed with her down the Clyde.

Despite the auspicious first journey, matters took a turn for the worse. *QE2*'s sea trials were due to start on 4 December 1968; but because of problems with oil seeping onto the water circuits, turbines malfunctioning and finishing work taking longer than expected, these were delayed until 23 December. Cunard employees and their families were asked to join the ship to act as passengers, so that the ship and crew could be 'tested' to ensure that everything would be perfect for the world's media, who were due to board at Las Palmas. This included testing all the rooms and beds, use all the public facilities and reporting back on any problems or

Lunch

Queen Elizabeth 2, Britannia Restaurant
Monday, May 5, 1969

Dinner

For your convenience the menus for both lunch and dinner are shown

Chef's Suggested Menu
Chilled Grapefruit Juice
Potage Longchamps
Baked Fresh Haddock, Claudine
Calf's Liver Saute, Bercy
Brussels Sprouts
French Fried Potatoes
Compote of Fruit with
Whipped Cream

Recommended Wines
Pouilly Fuisse 1964
Medoc

Juices
Grapefruit, Orange

Appetisers
Salade Creole, Choufleur à la
Grecque, Bismarck Herrings,
Continental Sausage

Soups
Consommé Mikado
Potage Longchamps

Fish
Baked Fresh Haddock, Claudine
Cold: Seafood Salad, Mayonnaise

Omelettes
Plain, Tomato

Entree
Calf's Liver, Saute, Bercy

Grill
Entrecote Steak, Forestiere

Joint
Roast Leg and Loin of Pork, Savoury
and Apple Sauce

Vegetables
Brussels Sprouts
Braised Spanish Onions

Farinaceous
Ravioli al Sugo

Potatoes
French Fried, Roast

Cold Buffet
Roast Ribs and Sirloin of Beef,
Raifort; Roast Duckling, Apple
Sauce; London Pressed Beef
Roast Chicken; Veal and Ham Pie

Salads
Lettuce and Tomato, Belgian Endive
Parmentier
(Choice of Dressings)

Sweets
Blackcurrant Pie, Fruit Compote
with Whipped Cream

Ice Cream
Vanilla, Strawberry, Tutti-Frutti

Cheese Board

Fresh Fruit

Tea (Hot or Iced)
Coffee (Hot or Iced)

Vin Blanc or Vin Rouge
Red Burgundy (Chapeau Rouge)
Large Carafe 7/6; Small Carafe 3/9;
Per Glass 1/3
Red Burgundy (Chapeau Rouge)
Large Carafe 12/-; Small Carafe 6/-;
Per Glass 2/-
White Burgundy (Bourgogne Aligote)
Large Carafe 12/-; Small Carafe 6/-;
Per Glass 2/-

Chef's Suggested Menu
Rouleaux of Foie Gras
Crème d'Asperges
Poached Suprème of Halibut
Dieppoise
Mixed Grill
Buttered French Beans
Persillées Potatoes
Coupe Andalouse

Recommended Wines
Moet and Chandon 1962
La Mission Haut Brion 1962

Your individual selection of wine may be
purchased from our comprehensive wine
list

Passengers on special diets are
especially invited to make known their
requirements to the Head Waiter

Speciality foods for infants are
available for ready service on request

Juices
Tomato, Apple

Appetisers
Chilled Honeydew Melon,
Rouleaux of Foie Gras
Eggs Tartare

Soups
Consommé Jockey Club
Crème d'Asperges

Fish
Poached Suprème of Halibut,
Dieppoise

Entree
Beefsteak Saute, Strogonoff

Roast
Roast Ribs and Sirloin of Beef,
Raifort (Yorkshire Pudding)

Grill
Mixed Grill

Vegetables
Buttered French Beans
Green Peas

Farinaceous
Noodles, Alsacienne

Potatoes
Château, Persillées

Cold Buffet
Selection of Assorted Cold Cuts

Salads
Romaine Lettuce, Cole Slaw
(Choice of Dressings)

Sweets
Pineapple Shortcake
Coupe Andalouse

Ice Cream
Vanilla, Raspberry

Cheese Board

Fresh Fruit

Tea (Hot or Iced)
Coffee (Hot or Iced)

Hotel Manager
J. R. Smith

Executive Chef
A. H. E. Townshend

Above: The Lunch and Dinner menus for Monday, 5 May 1969.

Right: The daily programme for QE2's first commercial sailing on Friday, 2 May 1969. The Virginia McKenna film *Ring of Bright Water* was shown in the theatre. QE2 left for New York at 9.30p.m.

faults that were found, so John Brown's and Cunard could sort them out before paying passengers arrived. However, when the Cunard employees arrived, they were horrified at what they found. The lower class cabins and crew cabins were unfinished and the whole place was a mess! The employees and crew spent the time between boarding and arriving at Las Palmas cleaning up and trying to make as much of the ship as complete as possible.

Captain W. E. Warwick and his Ship's Company welcome you on board

A special folder to hold your Daily Programmes, newspapers and other souvenirs of this Maiden Voyage, will be placed in your rooms

Table Reservations

Table Reservations for the Britannia Restaurant may be arranged with the Restaurant Manager, Port Side Forward of the Double Room, Upper Deck
Passengers who have made advance Table Reservations will find their Table Reservation Cards in their rooms

Meal Times
Britannia Restaurant

	Main Sitting	Late Sitting
Breakfast at	8.00 a.m.	9.00 a.m.
Luncheon at	12.15 p.m.	1.30 p.m.
Dinner at	6.30 p.m.	7.45 p.m.

Parents are advised that a separate Daily Programme is published for children

Your six-channel Radio Receiver will be programmed as follows:--
Channel 1: Background Music
Channel 2: Light Classical Music
Channel 3: News Broadcast every hour on the hour
Channel 4: B.B.C. Radio One
Channel 5: B.B.C. Radio Two
Channel 6: B.B.C. Radio Three

10.00 a.m.	Theatre Bar open	Upper Deck
10.30 a.m.	George Haley and his Orchestra	Double Room
10.30 a.m.	The Anna Dell Trio	Theatre Bar
10.30 a.m.	Discotheque with Diana and Ming	736 Club

12.30 p.m. **R.M.S ''Queen Elizabeth 2'' sails for Le Havre and New York**
A commentary on Southampton Water will be broadcast to the open decks, The Look Out and the Double Room
To enable passengers to watch the sailing of ''Queen Elizabeth 2'' Lunch will be served at:-
12.45 p.m. (Main Sitting) 2.15 p.m. (Late Sitting)

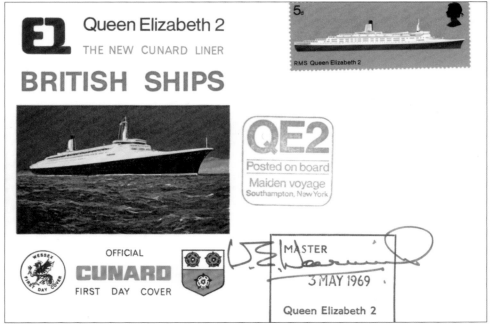

This page: A selection of different first day covers and advert postcards for her maiden voyage and pre-maiden voyage cruises.

CUNARD CRUISES 1970

Fares from £45

WELCOME
QUEEN ELIZABETH II
to The Rock

★

DIALDAS

175, Main Street
OMEGA & TISSOT
Official Agents.

FRIDAY, APRIL 24, 1970.   PRICE: FOURPENCE.

GIBRALTAR CHRONICLE

THE PAPER WITH NO POLITICAL BIAS
Vol. CCXLVI. No. 39,618.   FIRST PUBLISHED 1801.

DIALDAS

175, Main Street

★

OMEGA WATCHES
TISSOT WATCHES
ESTEE LAUDER COSMETICS
SAMSONITE LUGGAGE

Jewellery, Objets d'Art,
Table Linen, etc.

Trinidad rebels demand amnesty

PORT OF SPAIN, Thursday—In Trinidad, where security forces have arrested more Black Power leaders, talks are in progress between the government and rebel army units. One of the Black Power leaders detained is described as the head of the movement's national joint action committee.

Victor Feather calls for action on unemployment

LONDON, Thursday — The leader of Britain's trade unions, Mr Victor Feather, has called for a drive to reduce unemployment.

He was speaking after the news that the number of people out of work in Britain in April, more than 600,000, was the highest April total since 1948.

The rebels have demanded an amnesty, but the problem for the Prime Minister, Dr. Eric Williams, is whether he can come to terms with them without losing face and risking more violence.

Loyal troops still patrol the capital, Port of Spain, and although the aftermath of the looting and violence can be seen everywhere, the streets now seem quieter.

An American Navy task force of five ships has arrived off Trinidad and is anchored outside territorial waters. American small arms were flown in last night.

In London a Foreign Office spokesman said Britain will also send arms to help the Trinidad

QUEEN ELIZABETH 2 ARRIVES TODAY

THE Cunarder Queen Elizabeth 2 makes her first call at Gibraltar today with 1,700 passengers aboard — the largest number carried since she went into service a year ago. The QE 2 will be greeted by the Royal Navy with the Flag Officer Gibraltar, Rear Admiral Rodney Sturdee, flying his flag in HMS Lincoln, by RAF Hunters from North Front flying past and the Band of the 3rd. Battalion Royal Regiment of Fusiliers playing her into dock at the North Mole.

CUNARD *QE2* DAY
Saturday, November 7th
D U R B A N   T U R F   C L U B

Far left: The brochure for her first year's cruising season.

Above: In that first season, QE2 visited many different ports for the very first time. Each visit drew huge crowds and created great media interest, even in ports as small as Gibraltar.

Left: The Durban Turf Club held a series of horse races on the day QE2 arrived there.

Even at night, the world's newest liner looked magnificent.

Next page: As originally built, QE2 was designed to carry cars in her garage, with a capacity for about twenty vehicles.

Queen's Room: Garden/lounge by day, nightclub by night. Sculpted head of Queen Elizabeth II at forward entrance. Spans entire width of ship and surrounded on two sides by windows open to the sea. Amazing open, "airy" feeling due to slotted, trellis-style ceiling, more than 100 plants. (First Class).

Shops: Midships on Boat Deck. Buy watches, radios, cameras, souvenirs, gifts, cigarettes, candy, drugs, toiletry, toys, stationery, haberdashery, perfumes and cosmetics here. Hair Salon on One Deck (largest afloat) also offers complete ladies' and men's services.

Bureau: Centre of passenger service operations. Two banks and a travel office nearby. Other services include complete medical/dental hospital, print shop that produces a daily newspaper at sea.

Double Room: An epic nightclub on Boat *and* Upper Decks with special aluminium staircase in between. Largest public room of any ship afloat. Holds 800, yet is surprisingly intimate. (Tourist Class).

Midships – Bar: Quiet, plush room furnished in rich greens and bronze. Brass sphere shows relationship of planets to earth and signs of zodiac. Has the air of a private club (First Class).

Libraries: Quarter Deck Library (First Class) and Upper Deck Library (Tourist Class) have a total of more than 10,000 books, magazines and newspapers and room for 100 people to relax, read or write in comfort. Stamps are available.

Cardroom: Has some of the ship's most luxurious décor. Walls and chairs lined in green suede, rosewood tables with baize tops and special ceiling spotlights to illuminate games. Panoramic window allows spectating without disturbing players. (First Class).

Elevators/Stairways: Twenty-two passenger elevators for quick access to ten of eleven public decks. Eight passenger stairways — marked "A" to "H", colour coded by handrail/carpet colour.

Open Decks/Pools/Bar: Six decks with more open deck space than any ship afloat. Observation platform on Signal Deck. Open sports areas on Sports Deck. Open promenade on Boat Deck. Sunning area on Upper Deck (Tourist Class). Large lido/bar/pool area on Quarter Deck (First Class). Pool and lido on One Deck (Tourist Class).

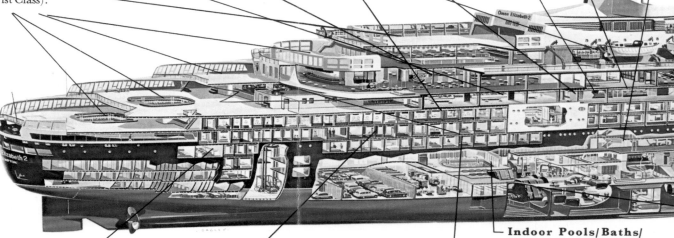

Launderettes: Two passenger launderettes (forward on One Deck; aft on Three Deck). Dry cleaning and valet service also available through Room Steward.

Staterooms: 904 rooms on five passenger decks, each with separate bath or shower, wall-to-wall carpeting, telephone, radio, roomy wardrobe and storage space.

Q4 Hideaway: Intimate, exclusive bar on Quarter Deck. "Hidden" location forward of Quarter Deck Pool, aft of Queen's Room (behind stage/dance floor). (First Class).

Indoor Pools/Baths/Gymnasium: Six Deck Pool (First Class) has Turkish bath (three different degree rooms). Seven Deck Pool (Tourist Class) has Swedish sauna and gymnasium. Both have massage tables.

Columbia Restaurant: eats 470. Lovely views of he sea. Unusual modern able table lamps, tinted bronze creens make it intimate nd festive. Ship-launching apestry opposite entrance. First Class).

Theatre/Theatre Bar: Seats 513. Used as theatre, cinema, conference room, interdenominational church (separate synagogue on Three Deck). Adjacent Theatre Bar (Tourist Class) offers cabaret entertainment, combos for dancing.

Coffee Shop: Offers coffee and ice cream confections during the day. Booths and special area with tables face sea. Adjacent is the "Juke Box" – with coin games, music and "crazy" mirrors – for the younger set.

Grill Room: Sophisticated, elegant restaurant with direct access by elevator or circular stairway through its own intimate bar. Most elegant "feel" of any room on ship. Restaurant seats 100 in specially designed chairs by Mies van der Rohe. Four statues represent air, earth, fire and water, are made of things from the sea. (First Class).

Britannia Restaurant: Seats 790 passengers with views of open sea in atmosphere and elegance of much smaller room. Six-foot-high sculpted Britannia figurehead at forward entrance; wooden ship models of Persia and Britannia (first Cunard ships to sail the Atlantic). (Tourist Class).

736 Casino: While the Queen is between ports, the casino offers games of Dice, Blackjack and Roulette. Has sizeable bar with good views of tables.

Bridge: Filled with modern navigational equipment, including a Ferranti computer that figures the safest, most comfortable route and checks *food* inventory. (Special tours arranged through the Bureau.)

Lookout Bar: On Upper Deck, right under the Bridge, the ship's furthest forward-looking public room. Panoramic windows for sea-view cocktails. Swinging discotheque at night. Usually *the* late-action spot. (Tourist Class).

Open Decks/Pools/Bar: Six decks with more open deck space than any ship afloat. Observation platform on Signal Deck. Open sports areas on Sports Deck. Open promenade on Boat Deck. Sunning area on Upper Deck (Tourist Class). Large lido/bar/pool area on Quarter Deck (First Class). Pool and lido on One Deck (Tourist Class).

Engine and Boiler Rooms: Largest, most powerful of any passenger ship. Supply enough light, heat and power to run a big city the size of Salt Lake City, Utah.

Midships Lobby: Only circular lobby with two-level seating afloat. On Two Deck, perfect place to start ship tour. Information desk, principal stairways/elevators just aft. (First Class).

Staterooms: 904 rooms on five passenger decks, each with separate bath or shower, wall-to-wall carpeting, telephone, radio, roomy wardrobe and storrage space.

Kitchens: Include oven that makes 200 individual soufflés at once, separate kosher kitchen, elevators to storerooms eight decks below. Here, 12½ tons of beef, 200 pounds of caviar, one ton of lobsters, ten tons of fresh fruit, one and a half tons of duck, a mile of sausages and more than 2,500 bottles of wine are stored.

CUNARD

In addition, the engines broke down en-route to Las Palmas. It took a while to root out the problem, but it was found that it was the effect of steam excitation on the turbine blades in stages 7 and 8. This was a very minor turbine fault which should have been picked up at the beginning of the sea trials. Once the Press boarded the ship, the problems with *QE2*'s turbines and the unfinished work on the world's most luxurious liner, that had been proclaimed as a destination in itself, started being broadcast to the world. It was a public relations disaster and one that Cunard could ill afford.

The turbine problems caused havoc with *QE2*'s maiden voyage as well. This, and all future voyages had to be cancelled until it was fixed. Cunard refused to accept the ship from the shipbuilders until all the problems had been fixed, and also refused to pay John Brown's (now part of Upper Clyde Shipbuilders) the outstanding sums for the ship. The problems eventually took many months and a lot of heartache to sort out, preventing the new liner from entering service.

Queen Elizabeth 2 finally made her maiden voyage with Cunard on 22 April 1969, with a short 'shakedown' cruise to the Canary Islands. Her officers and crew could at last test her at sea to see what the new liner was capable of.

Queen Elizabeth visited the liner that bore her name on the eve of its maiden voyage. She inspected the ship and had lunch in the Grill Room. The maiden voyage of *Queen Elizabeth 2* was a complete success. She arrived triumphantly at New York and captured hearts on both sides of the Atlantic. Aircraft few past and the fireboats sprayed their jets to welcome her to New York. The *QE2*'s purpose was slightly different from her predecessors – although still an ocean greyhound, she would also be as comfortable as a cruise ship. She would be a floating resort, a playground, an escape. She became a haven for those well-known people who needed to 'get away from it all'. Those who would rather spend five days being pampered and arrive like an icon, rather than spend ten hours cooped up in a jet and arrive looking bedraggled and tired. *QE2* was luxury at its best and catered for a niche market.

Included in this luxury were items of artwork, specially commissioned for the ship. Cunard had always been careful about respecting and maintaining its heritage and tradition. Equally, the company was not scared to mix the old with the new. Items like the bust of Queen Elizabeth, by Oscar Nemon, which stood in the Queens Room, the Royal Standards which had hung on the original *Queen Mary* and *Queen Elizabeth*, and models of the *Britannia* and *Persia* which stood in glass cases in the Britannia Restaurant; mix with new items such as the 21ft by 7ft tapestry of *QE2*'s launch by Helen Banynina, and the Four Element statues by Janine Jane in the Grill Room. One of *QE2*'s most prized possessions was the solid silver Boston Cup, given to Cunard's *Britannia* in 1841 by the residents of Boston when they cut her out of the ice in order that she could continue her mail voyage.

By 1971, Cunard had been sold to a British Company, Trafalgar House for £26 million. And in that same year *Franconia* and *Carmania* were sold. So until Cunard's new ships *Cunard Adventurer* and *Cunard Ambassador* were completed, the *QE2* had the responsibility of carrying the Cunard name and reputation around the world.

On 17 May 1972 a radio message came into the *QE2*'s radio room. The message read 'Threat of explosion to destroy ship unless demand cash payment met. Explosives set on six separate decks. Authorities advise take all necessary precautions. Two accomplices may be on board. Monitor all cables and telephone messages.' Earlier in the day, there had also been a threatening telephone call from a man demanding $530,000 or he would blow up the ship.

Cunard and the Ministry of Defence met to discuss the situation. The ransom would be paid, but also bomb disposal personnel would be parachuted onto the ship to try and locate the devices. The suspect packages were found to be two suitcases on the boat deck and four large containers on the car deck. After an exhaustive search, no bombs were found. But on 18 May, the Cunard offices in New York received a letter telling them where the ransom should be taken to. Although the ransom was deposited at the designated spot, no one ever came to collect it; and the ransom was returned to Cunard. It was found that it was a hoax phone call and the man was arrested.

Each of the four bomb disposal experts who risked their lives on the ship received The Queen's Commemoration for Brave Conduct.

A couple of years later (1974) the film *Juggernaut* was made. Although a work of fiction, the facts are very close to the story of the bomb threats on board *QE2*. The story takes place on board the luxury liner *Britannic* (incidentally, the name of an old Cunard White Star ship), which contained a series of bombs contained within oil drums placed aboard. The stars of the film were Richard Harris, Omar Sharif and Anthony Hopkins.

Going back to 1973, the *QE2* was chartered for two cruises to commemorate the 25th Anniversary of the founding of Israel. This caused quite a controversy, and later it was found out that President Anwar Sadat of Egypt personally thwarted an attempt by President Gadaffi of Libya to torpedo the *QE2*.

By the early 1970s, QE2 was so popular that extra cabins were installed aboard. These penthouse suites ruined her simple, clean lines but over the past thirty or so years, have generated huge income for Cunard. Outward bound from Southampton on 2 June 1973 at 9.30p.m.

In 1974, while cruising from New York, QE2 suffered a catastrophic failure of three boilers and her 1,600 passengers had to be rescued by the Norwegian Sea Venture on 5 April. The passengers were taken to New York via Bermuda. Officers of the Sea Venture wave as they depart the QE2.

In 1974, while in mid-Atlantic on a cruise from New York to the Caribbean, QE2 suffered catastrophic boiler failure on three boilers and her entire complement of 1,600 passengers had to be rescued by the Norwegian vessel *Sea Venture*. They returned back to New York via Bermuda.

The *QE2* made her first round the world voyage in 1975. During this voyage she broke two world records. The first was when she became the largest ship to transit the Panama Canal; and the second was that she paid the highest toll fee for a ship to cross the Canal.

1976 was a busy year for Cunard. Two new passenger ships were added to the fleet, *Cunard Countess* and *Cunard Conquest*. At 17,000 tons they were small compared to *QE2* but they carried their passengers in total luxury. This brought the Cunard passenger fleet list to three ships. Then Trafalgar House, who owned Cunard, decided to purchase twelve fruit-carrying ships. These were also added to the Cunard fleet, and given names with the traditional Cunard –ia endings, such as *Servia, and Carmania*.

Also in July 1976, fire broke out on the *Queen Elizabeth 2*. She had just started a Transatlantic voyage and was passing Bishop's Rock Lighthouse, when fire was detected. She turned round and headed back for Southampton. Her boiler room was damaged and she had to undergo repairs.

1978 saw *QE2* arrive in New Jersey for both external and internal refits. The Bethlehem Steel Corporation carried out the seventeen day overhaul. Pre-assembled luxury penthouses were added just behind the Bridge (called the Queen Mary and Queen Elizabeth suites, these were split level). The restaurants had an overhaul too. The Britannia Restaurant was revamped into five smaller dining areas, collectively known as Tables of the World. Each area took on a different place, e.g. the Londoner (Olde English), Florentine (Italian), Flamenco (Spanish), Parisienne (French) and Oriental. Everything in these themed restaurants reflected the country, right down to the waiters' uniforms! New kitchens were added to cope with the additional meals. The staterooms were given a new look and the teenagers' area also had a games room added.

During 1982, the *QE2* started her long association with Concorde. The ultimate in luxury, Concorde, could travel at twice the speed of sound and her average flight time between London and New York was 3½ hours. Instead of going against one another, *QE2* and Concorde teamed up to provide the most luxurious way to cross the Atlantic. This appealed to the rich and famous because they could fly quickly to their meetings on one continent and return in pure luxury and pampering to the other continent.

Passing down Southampton Water, with the Pilot boat in attendance.

Anchored in October 1973, QE2 is showing some signs of a hard summer season, with rust streaks on her otherwise immaculate paintwork.

Clockwise from top left: QE2 in the King George V graving dock in Southampton during 1979. She is receiving a much needed paint job. The blue paint being applied to her keel is anti-fouling paint, used to prevent marine growth that would slow her down.

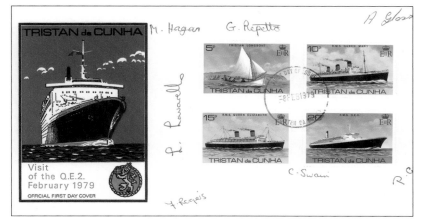

Above, left and right: Two postal covers from QE2's first visit to the remote island of Tristan da Cunha, signed by many of the local inhabitants.

Right: Japan was, and still is, a very good market for Cunard. This image, originally issued as a postcard, shows her at Yokohama.

In 1982, Argentina invaded the Falkland Islands and QE2, as well as many other ships of Britain's mercantile marine, was commandeered by the Royal Navy. Hastily converted to a troopship, with helicopter decks built on her bow and stern, QE2 was loaded with Marines, RAMC and Commandos and sailed via Sierra Leone for the war zone.

FALKLANDS CONFLICT

My own memory of the Falklands conflict is of sitting on a small pleasure boat on the River Thames as an eleven-year-old when I heard on the BBC news that the *QE2* was being called up for active service. I clearly remember the soldiers being embarked on board, and Rod Stewart's *Sailing* becoming the defining song of the era.

The *Queen Elizabeth 2* was requisitioned on 4 May 1982. Her purpose would be a troop carrier and for this she would need a military-style refit. Because of her speed, she could move massive amounts of troops faster than most naval ships. On 5 May, work began. Her stern decks were cut back to provide a helicopter landing pad, and her quarter deck was extended forward so that another helicopter landing pad could be installed there. Constructed behind her Bridge was a new radio room. Her beautiful interior fittings and furnishings were removed, as well as her works of art. Her floors were covered with hardboard to protect her carpets. The cinema was turned into a briefings room, and the Double Room became a soldiers' lounge, and the exclusive shopping arcade became a Naafi. The Tables of the World Restaurant was the soldiers' mess, and the Grill Rooms were reserved for Officers.

The conversion work also included enabling the liner to take stores and equipment down to the Falklands for use during the combat. Items such as Landrovers, rations and fuel were sent down with the ship. The ship also carried extra lifejackets.

The crew were given the option to volunteer for service, as they knew best how to operate the ship. Out of the 1,000 crew who volunteered, 650 were chosen, including 33 stewardesses.

On 13 May 1982, the great liner *Queen Elizabeth 2* pulled out of her berth at Southampton to take her precious souls to war. The troops on board were from the Fifth Infantry Brigade, made up of Gurkha Rifles, Welsh Guards and Scots Guards as well as soldiers from other branches of the Forces. *QE2* was on her way to join some old Cunard and P&O friends, including *Canberra,* and Cunard's *Atlantic Conveyor, Cunard Countess, and Luminetta.* With a complete blackout and radio silence in force, QE2 sailed into the sunset. No one knew where she was, and with black bin liners covering her portholes the soldiers were unsure of her location too. Sailing far from land, it was not until she arrived off Sierra Leone that anyone knew her location. David Yates, an RAMC Medic, remembered a Russian spy trawler off shore broadcasting the hitherto location of the ship. With radar switched off, as *QE2* approached the Falklands in dense fog, it was deemed necessary to switch this back on.

R.M.S. Queen Elizabeth 2
Monday 17th May 1982

Lunch

Orange Fruit Cup

Cream of Tomato Soup

Veal and Pork Loaf in Pastry,
with Mushroom Sauce

Corned Round and Brisket of Beef
with Vegetables

Lima Beans

Creamed Potatoes

Assorted Cold Cuts

Mixed Salad with Dressings

Rhubarb Pie with Custard

Cheese and Biscuits

Rolls and Butter

Tea or Coffee

I.S.

Above: Some of QE2's crew and survivors from HMS *Coventry*, on QE2's forward helicopter flight deck.

Top: Because of her importance, QE2 never sailed into the war zone itself, but sailed for South Georgia where she unloaded her troops onto *Canberra* and other vessels and then she sailed for home with the injured from HMS *Coventry*, *Ardent* and *Antelope*. Here, she returns to a hero's welcome, escorted by HMY *Britannia*, on 11 June 1982.

Left: An on board menu from her Falklands trip. The soldiers on board ate well, which was probably not a great consolation for those who travelled by converted North Sea ferry.

Suddenly, many icebergs popped up on screen, quite a few of them large enough to sink the ship. It was a lucky escape.

The time spent on the journey was put to good use and many thousands of rounds of ammunition were expended on target practice by the soldiers. Two heavy machine guns were installed on the Bridge wings to help repel enemy aircraft.

QE2 arrived near the Falklands, sailed past and made for South Georgia and transferred her troops and stores. It was deemed to be inappropriate to let her too near the conflict as she bore the name of the present Queen. Instead, *Canberra* was used to take troops into the war zone. Cunard suffered one loss during this conflict and that was when an Exocet missile hit *Atlantic Conveyor*.

Queen Elizabeth 2 arrived at her destination, Cumberland Bay (about 200 miles from the Falklands), where she was greeted by the *Canberra*, HMS *Endurance* and the North Sea Ferry *Norland*. QE2's soldiers disembarked, and war casualties from HMS *Coventry*, HMS *Ardent* and HMS *Antelope* were loaded onto the ship. Then she was moved out of Cumberland Bay, as she was still in an area where she could be attacked, and she set sail for home.

The QE2 arrived triumphantly back home at Southampton on 11 June 1982. She had travelled over 14,000 miles in two months and tremendously helped the war effort. Near Southampton she was greeted by Her Royal Highness, The Queen Mother on the Royal Yacht *Britannia* (another John Brown's built ship) as well as one of the largest flotillas of small ships ever to be seen in the port. As the QE2 arrived at Southampton, a sea of banners of 'welcome' greeted her and her heroes home.

Opposite above: Thousands gathered to witness the returning vessel and her victorious arrival at Southampton was broadcast around the world.

Opposite below: Soon afterwards, as part of the huge refit designed to remove all traces of her short but illustrious naval career, QE2 sported a fetching grey livery.

Above left: In Southampton Water, 1983.

Above middle: At Yokohama, 1983.

Above right: Photographed in the English Channel while approaching Southampton. Her mooring lines are already out.

Below left: Approaching her home port.

Below right: QE2 makes her first approach to her New York pier while in her new grey livery.

Above: The Midships bar.

Above left: The Tables of the World restaurant was bright and modern with five distinct dining areas serving French, Spanish, Oriental, Italian and English meals.. The Q4 room was also replaced with a new Club Lido, which had mirrored walls.

Left: Her Double Room was still the focal point of events aboard.

Above left: Despite losing much space to the penthouse block in 1973, QE2 is still blessed with a huge expanse of deck area.

Above middle: Unfortunately, her grey paintwork, while stunning when new, couldn't stand the ravages of the Atlantic, as this rust streaked QE2 shows. Southampton, late 1983.

Above right: Between 28 November and 12 December 1983, QE2 entered dry dock at HAPAG-Lloyd Werft for a refit and repaint to her traditional livery.

Below right: On 8 July 1984, Queen Elizabeth 2 made her 500th voyage.

Below left: A Christmas card from 1984 for use aboard.

Next page: During numerous refits, QE2 lost such things as her garage but still retained her kennels, located forward of the funnel.

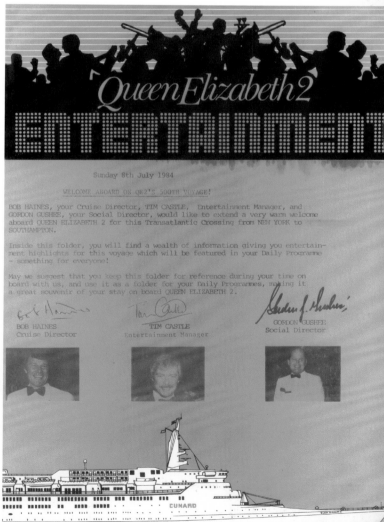

1 Outdoor pool
2 Lido Magrodome indoor/
  outdoor centre with pool
3 Club Lido
4 Deck tennis
5 Launderette
6 Double Down Bar
7 Florist's Shop
8 Double Room
9 Shopping Arcade

10 Club Lido buffet
11 Queens Room
12 Golden Door Health Spa
13 Ship's Control Room
14 Midships Bar
15 Theatre Bar
16 Columbia Restaurant
17 Kennels
18 530-seat Theatre/Cinema
   with balcony

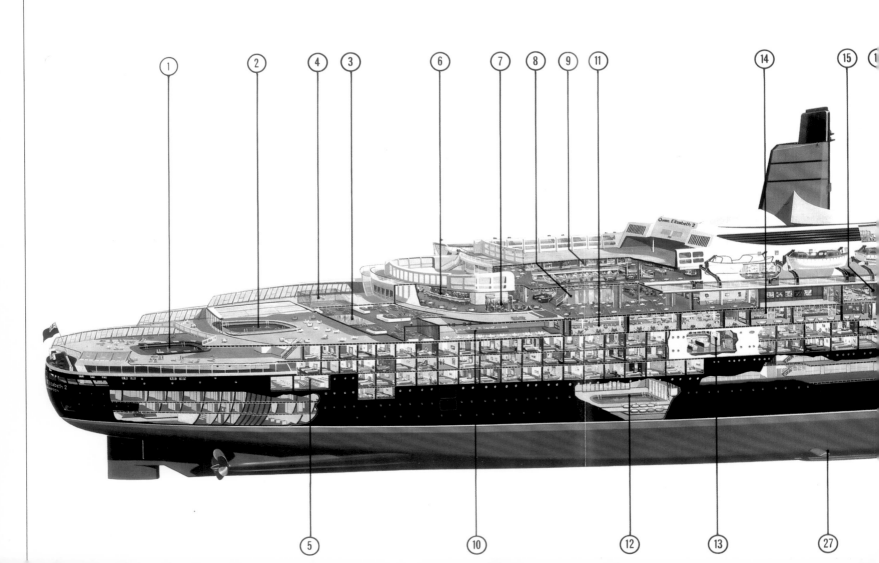

: A CITY AT SEA

en's Area with
a and creche
ps Lobby
s Grill Bar
s Grill
e Penthouse Suites
e navigation dome
eck jogging track
e Room
zers

28 Indoor pool and Gymnasium
29 Printing Works
30 Tables of the World Restaurant
31 Queen Elizabeth Suite
32 Car Lift
33 Garage
34 Bridge
35 Promenade Deck
36 Crew accommodation and
rest facilities

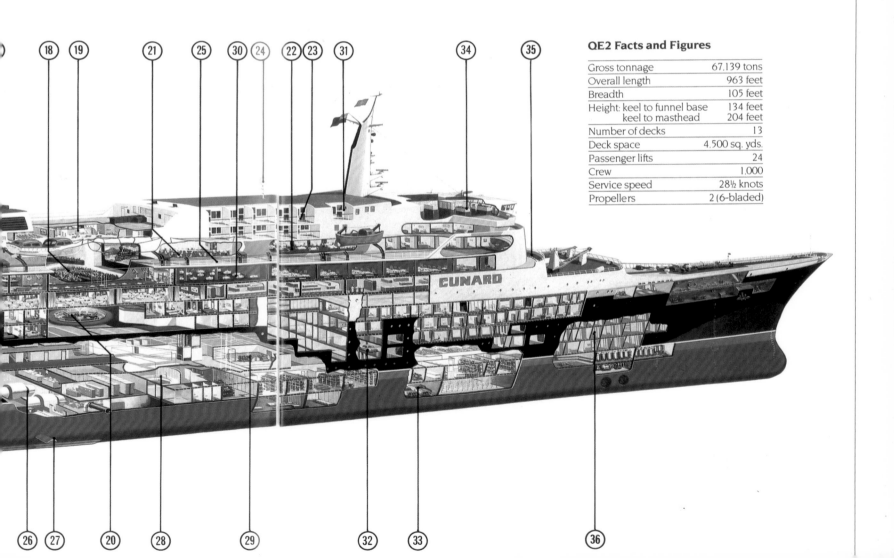

QE2 Facts and Figures

Gross tonnage	67,139 tons
Overall length	963 feet
Breadth	105 feet
Height: keel to funnel base	134 feet
keel to masthead	204 feet
Number of decks	13
Deck space	4,500 sq. yds.
Passenger lifts	24
Crew	1,000
Service speed	28½ knots
Propellers	2 (6-bladed)

Chapter 6

ELIZABETH'S CARNIVAL

Queen Elizabeth 2 had been in service almost two decades when she experienced her most major refit. Just prior to this on 25 October 1986, she performed the last ever crossing of the Atlantic by Cunard steamship, as her refit would see her powerplant converted from steam to diesel. Cunard was looking to the long-term future of the *QE2* and by converting her to diesel and giving her a refit, it would ensure that the ship would keep running soundly for another few decades.

The upgrade of the *QE2* started with a meeting between Cunard and possible companies who would tender for the refitting works. Of the companies invited to tender, only Lloyd Werft in Bremerhaven and Blohm und Voss in Hamburg, could match the price and had the facilities that Cunard required. After further negotiations Lloyd Werft were awarded the contract on 24 October 1985.

Just over a year later, on 26 October 1986, *QE2* arrived at the shipyard, ready for her refit. It was envisaged that this refit would take 179 days to complete. Unlike her construction, her parts would not come from all over Britain, but from all over Europe.

QE2's funnel was the first item to disappear in order to gain access to the engine rooms. Then parts of the sides were opened to allow parts to

be manoeuvred inside. A huge floating crane hoisted the parts, such as the generators into place. Toward the end of the refit, *QE2* was capped with a new funnel. It was a more traditional funnel than its predecessor, but necessary because it housed nine new exhaust pipes.

During the same refit, eight new penthouse suites were fitted; and because of the additional passengers, the Queen's Grill had to be enlarged. The Queen's Grill bar also had to have a revamp. The Tables of the World Restaurant was redesigned and called the Mauretania Restaurant. The Mauretania Restaurant was styled in the Art Deco style and had a painting of the old *Mauretania* in it. Both the Princess Grill and the Columbia Restaurant were given a makeover too.

The Double Room had also been modified. The stairway between the two levels was changed, and the shopping arcade on the top floor was extended. The Yacht Club bar was also added during this refit. This had a maritime theme with ship models and a transparent glazed piano. An upgrade of the sports facilities was added, including an automatic golf unit – the first of its kind at sea.

The *QE2* could boast a computer learning centre after this refit, where passengers can learn new computer skills. A new boardroom was also

Above left: In October 1986, QE2 made her last voyage under steam power, bringing to an end 146 years of Cunard steamships. A menu cover from her last steam voyage.

Above right: The engine room spaces were cleared in anticipation of the new diesel engines. Operating and fuel costs were reduced by 40 per cent and the ship's working life extended to (at the time) another twenty years.

added, which can accommodate small conferences or private cocktail parties.

The Queen's Award for Export Achievements was awarded to the *Queen Elizabeth 2* in 1987. This award was for an increase in export earnings which is outstanding for the product.

Over the next few years, QE2 had a few interesting incidents. In 1992, she hit some uncharted rocks at speed just off Martha's Vineyard. Then, on 11 September 1995, she ran in the path of Hurricane Luis on a westbound transatlantic voyage. It was during this storm that a 90ft wave smashed into the ship. The reason the height of this wave was known was that it's crest was level with the Bridge. The wave hit the ship causing her to roll severely. Many on board thought that they would not survive the monster wave, but in true *QE2* style, she righted herself and ploughed on through the storm. The wave had broken windows on the Bridge, knocked out navigational equipment and hospitalised passengers, but at least they had survived!

On 2 January 1996, QE2 marked her 4 millionth mile at sea. During 1996, Trafalgar House decided to sell Cunard. Because Cunard was a private company now and the Articles which prohibited the company being sold to British interests only were not applicable any more, Trafalgar House decided to sell Cunard to the Kvaerner construction and shipbuilding group, of Norway. For the first time in Cunard's history the line would be wholly owned by a foreign company.

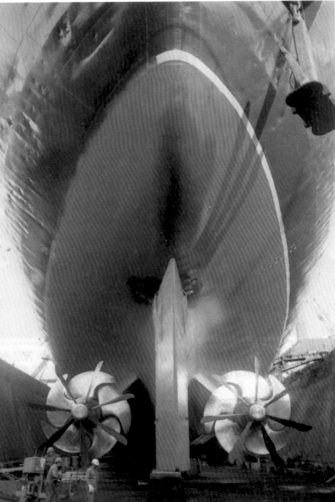

Top left: QE2 in dry dock, minus her funnel, which was to be replaced with a new design, visible bottom right. *Canberra*, that other famous British cruise ship, is also in dock.

Top right: Parts of her new decks being lifted aboard, ready for welding into place.

Far left: Installing the Cunard lion rampant logo into the floor of the swimming pool was a painstakingly long task.

Left: New propeller blades were fitted too.

Clockwise from top left:

The Double Room was converted into a Grande Lounge, with a shopping promenade installed too.

The Columbia restaurant was refurbished too.

As was the Queen's Room.

While the cabins took on a new, more modern look. This is Cabin 8001, a suite with a balcony.

Kvaerner quickly reduced Cunard's passenger fleet to just two ships, *QE2* and *Vistafjord*. *Cunard Princess* was sold to MSC, and *Cunard Countess* was sold to Awani Cruises. *Sagafjord* was originally sold to TransOcean Cruises, but then onto Saga Cruises as *Saga Rose*.

The Carnival Corporation, which already owned some of the world's major cruise lines, became interested in Cunard when Kvaerner hinted the line would be for sale. This would add a luxury line to their fleets, and help them become one of the largest cruise ship owners in the world. In May 1998, Kvaerner sold Cunard to the Carnival Corporation. At the time, this was what Cunard really needed after almost a decade of lack of investment. Carnival had the capital to invest, but it also had the cruise line expertise needed to turn Cunard from a failing company into a twenty-first century icon. On the other hand, Cunard had established an enviable reputation and clientele; not to mention an air of exclusivity. Carnival paid well over the odds for what was a two ship line, but with

Clockwise from top:
The Double Down Bar Aft was fitted with a Dampa ceiling in curved aluminium.

With new deck areas in place, QE2 was as good as new again and ready for twenty years more service. The refit had cost a massive £90M, not much short of the price of a new vessel.

Still with work to do, QE2 is on her sea trials with her new diesel engines fitted. Containers, rather than deckchairs, litter the decks.

In 1991, QE2 visited Cunard's home port of Liverpool for the very first time. Berthed in the middle of the river, it was a gala occasion and the Mersey ferries made constant trips to and from her all day long.

Entering New York, 1986.

the *QE2* and *Vistafjord* came an unrivalled almost-160 years of history, tradition and goodwill. *QE2* was the only ship regularly ploughing the North Atlantic and controlled a niche market – transatlantic crossings. Many cruise lines in the late twentieth century only ventured across oceans on repositioning cruises from one continent to another. *QE2* was built to take on the worst that the North Atlantic could throw at her, and she regularly did!

On the thirtieth anniversary of her maiden voyage in May 1969, *QE2* decided to give Southampton a salute of her very own. She sat at her berth and her ship's foghorn sounded thirty long and very loud blasts to the city that had been her home – one blast for each year of her service. Of course, with a foghorn that could be heard over ten miles away, not just Southampton heard the mighty *QE2* that day.

But Carnival already had plans to add a sister ship to the fleet for *Queen Elizabeth 2*. They first considered a design that they code-named *Q5*, but this idea for a ship never really got any further than the drawing board. Then, after a major rethink, the *Q6* project was announced. Q6 was to be another Queen, just like *Queen Elizabeth 2*, but larger and grander. Planned to be the world's largest ocean liner, she was to be, like every Queen before her, a ship of superlatives. However, world events were to intervene.

On 11 September 2001, the world changed with the terrorist attacks on the World Trade Center in New York. *QE2* had been on a transatlantic voyage between Southampton and New York with a very special young couple on board. Rebecca Warwick, daughter of Captain Ronald Warwick and grand-daughter of the late Captain Bill Warwick, was on board to marry her fiancé Chris Lacey. The ceremony would be performed on board *Queen Elizabeth 2* by Captain Warwick when the party reached New York. Unfortunately, events took a turn for the worse when the terrorist attack happened on the World Trade Centre and *QE2* was diverted to Boston. After lots of re-organisation and stress, a licence was issued in Boston for them to marry on board *Queen Elizabeth 2* on 4 October 2001.

QE2 was the first ship to return to her American home port after 9/11. When she arrived, a wreath was dropped into the water and her flag was lowered to half-mast. For many months her berth and its buildings had been used as an emergency management command centre for the World Trade Centre tragedy.

In 2004, the *QE2* was withdrawn from her transatlantic service to become a full-time cruise ship. She still performs some transatlantic voyages, but these are mainly left to her younger sister *Queen Mary 2*, which entered service in January of that year. There were many special events planned for both ships, not least of which was a tandem voyage of the Atlantic by two Cunard liners. Commodore Warwick also transferred over from *QE2* to *QM2* while the latter was being fitted out. With the introduction of *QM2*, the longest, widest and tallest ocean liner ever built, *QE2* now sails from Southampton to Europe, the Mediterranean and other destinations, and in the winter she undertakes her annual world cruise. Although in semi-retirement, she is still a very active member of the Cunard passenger shipping fleet!

With *QE2*'s large new sister, *Queen Mary 2* under construction, the Carnival Corporation announced in December 2001 that it was to build another new liner of roughly equal size to the *Queen Elizabeth 2* called *Queen Victoria* and she made a successful entry into service in December 2007 and was built at Fincantieri in Italy.

QE2 – THE FUTURE

Like all ships, *QE2* cannot go on forever. She has already been in service longer than any other Cunard ship; she has travelled more miles than any other Cunard ship, in fact many more miles than any other ship ever built. It was announced on 18 June 2007 that *QE2* had been sold for use as a floating hotel in Dubai. For the princely sum of $100M, Isthitmar, the investment arm of Dubai World, intends to berth her at the resort and return her to her 1969 glory, complete with recreated original interiors and furnishings. In November 2009, she will be opened to the public once more in the United Arab Emirates and will continue to give pleasure to millions as the most glamorous vessel afloat. It is hard to believe that 2008 is her final season as an ocean-going vessel, but she has escaped the breaker's torch after being driven onto some distant Indian or Pakistani beach, a fate which has befallen some glorious vessels of the 1950s, 1960s and 1970s in recent years. Cunard themselves achieved a price that was unheard of and at 2007 prices it represented four times what they would have received as scrap value for the venerable old lady

The final season of *QE2* has been tinged with sadness and many people are making their farewells to the ship. Sailing round Britain's coasts for the last time, many tens of thousands have come to say their goodbyes to this ship of superlatives. 2008 has also seen *QE2*'s last world cruise, had her sail transatlantic with her stablemates, a meeting of three Queens in Southampton and a series of cruises that culminate in her final voyage to Dubai in November 2008, with a huge party on the dockside and along the banks of the Solent for her final farewell to the port she has called home since 1969.

QE2 will, of course, be looked after in her new home, with much expense lavished on her and, no doubt, she will look fantastic with her original interiors refitted where practical, although the author will have to watch out for her original furnishings purchased over the years after various refits. Of course, Cunard could not let the name die and a new Cunard Queen will carry the name Queen Elizabeth, the third ship of the fleet to do so. She enters service in Autumn 2010.

CUNARD

Opposite, clockwise from top left:
Travelling up the North Sea, 2001. The view from the port docking wing.

The author greets Commodore Warwick aboard ship in 2001.

Iceberg ahead! Commodore Warwick keeps the ship on autopilot, just in case!

Two giants of Scottish engineering together.

Above: This painting of QE2 upon her maiden arrival to New York used to hang onboard QE2 in Captain Bill Warwick's day cabin and now resides in the author's home, having been purchased from his son, Commodore Ron Warwick.

TOW LINE

Above: Tow Line, the Moran Towing & Transportation Co. magazine dedicated their front cover to the vessel.

Opposite, clockwise from top left:
QE2's new sister and Commodore Warwick's last command before he retired, the first new ocean liner to be built since *Vistafjord* in 1974.

Queen Mary 2 in Southampton, January 2004.

2004 was a bumper year for Cunard fans when both QE2 and QM2 were in Southampton together for the first time. *(Nicholas Leach/Ships Monthly)*

QE2 alongside, Southampton, 2004. *(Nicholas Leach/Ships Monthly)*